LAUGHTER AND CRY

Writings of
Tearz Ayuen

Africa World Books Pty Ltd

A Note from the Publisher

The publisher wishes to acknowledge and thank Dr Douglas
H. Johnson for his invaluable help and support for Africa
World Books and its mission of preserving and promoting
African cultural and literary traditions and history. Dr Johnson
and fellow historians have been instrumental in ensuring
that African people remain connected to their past and their
identity. Africa World Books is proud to carry on this mission.

© Tearz Ayuen, 2020

ISBN: 978-0-6489291-6-1

Design and typesetting: Africa World Books

PART I

POLITICAL MATTERS

Nhial and Majak Leave Earth

February 4, 2013

IN THE YEAR 2099, MAJAK (INCUMBENT DEPUTY MINISTER OF DEFENSE) and Nhial (foreign affairs minister) die of old age, on the same day - December 31. They go straight to Hades. Hades lies between Heaven and Hell.

It is a sort of a way-station. Just like any other institution, it has policies - rules and regulations. Authorities in Hell, Heaven and Hades work hand in hand. Hades coordinates the activities. It keeps copies of the lists of those who are destined for heaven and Hell. Anyone who gets there has his or her name ticked and shown a room to wait for instructions - whether to proceed to Heaven or Hell.

Hades

Here, Nhial and Majak share a bed, because the place is congested as crowds keep coming from earth. This is because people are dying in wars, and others, of fatal man-made diseases created by European and American scientists just to reduce the overwhelming world populations, particularly the poor.

Nhial and Majak recognize a lot of South Sudanese they knew way back on earth, mostly those who let down South Sudan during and after the liberation struggle. These were those who collaborated with Khartoum butcher their own people in exchange of food. Some were those who broke away from the government and worked to destabilize South Sudan during its infancy.

Amongst the old buddies they meet in Hades are Kerubino Kuanyin Bol, Gabriel Tanginye, Peter Gatdet, George Athor, Bapiny Manytuil, Olony, Samuel Gai Tut, Akuot Atem and many others. Each one of them narrates why he is spending such a long time in Hades without going to Heaven or Hell.

As they chat, Nhial spots two elderly men seated on a mat made of reeds. "Oh my God, am I dreaming or is that Abel Alier and Joseph Lagu?" In unison, they reply "yes." Immediately, Majak wonders: "What happened? I thought they were in heaven, considering how they participated in the fight against Khartoum regimes."

The two chaps walk over to the elders and greet them. As the conversation gets interesting and deeper, Nhial chips in with a question in: "Uncles, we're so surprised that you two are still here, what happened? We thought you were in heaven." Being so old, Abel and Lagu say they can't remember what went down.

The truth is, being the senior and wiser figures in their region then, they had surprisingly gullibly allowed President Numeiri to drive a wedge between them. That is President Numeiri had them fight one another after he successfully made Dinka Bor cattle destroy Bari farms. Both Lagu and Alier failed to resolve the problem amicably, leaving it to escalate into wider political conflicts involving students, civil service and other societal groups in the South.

In the beginning, Lagu was the best leader. He tried his best to keep the rebellion strong and progressive. But he gave up in the middle of the revolt against Khartoum. He is a quitter. Besides, during his tenure as the Second President of the High Executive Council of the Southern Sudan Autonomous Region, Lagu got carried away by the goodies – including a big-breasted northern woman - offered to him by the then Khartoum regime, thus forgetting his people and their cause. To make matters worse and like Alier, he relocated to Khartoum. Their decisions and actions, in many ways, caused incalculable suffering amongst their people.

To cut the long story short, Nhial and Majak are summoned into the boss' office. The head of Hades, a huge, imposing dude with a scary scar on his left cheek, briefs them: "Boys, you're so lucky, you just got here and I have been instructed to ready you for an exit. I received a message from Heaven last night. It says your names have been screened and you were found sinless: you were good political leaders. You never got involved in corrupt practices. That's it, boys. Prepare for your entry to heaven. You've a couple of hours."

The two walk out of the room with faces shining with big smiles. Back in the dorm, they break the good news to their countrymen. Some express happiness for them. Others feel jealous. Tanginye is one of the guys who are unhappy about the good news. He gets up and begins to attack the two, verbally:

"How come you guys are going to Heaven? God must be crazy. That's not fair at all. You lazy dudes who let down South Sudanese.

You were always silent about critical issues affecting the common man. Particularly you, Nhial, as a Foreign Minister, what good things did you do? All you did was bragging, all day all night, bragging about academic papers. When Khartoum was committing atrocities, killing and destroying structures in the country, when your Sudanese counterpart was winning sympathizers using diplomatic war tactics, like a statue, you sat in your chair, doing what you do best – keeping quiet. You thought degrees and doctorates would work by themselves? You're the type of people whose actions drove me nuts and to rebel against Salva Kiir's government. Had I entered Juba with my commandos, I would have shot you in the ear. For you, Majak, who the hell do you think you are? Mister Parrot, do you really believe that you are without blemish; that you are going to Heaven? God must be kidding me. Let me count the bad things you did in South Sudan. One, you were involved in…"

Here scuffle erupts. One of Majak's supporters punches Tanginye in the mouth, prompting the two sides to get at each other like hungry lions. They cause a big scene. A Kenyan man is overheard saying, "Hawa watu wanapenda vita sana," loosely translated as: These people like fighting a lot.

Heaven

Majak and Nhial arrive at the Gates of Heaven. St. Paul and St. Peter are guarding the gates. "Hello, brethren. Welcome to Heaven. I'm your brother, St. Paul and my brother here is St. Peter. Identify yourselves, please."

As they undergo formal procedure, some people inside the walls of heaven begin to peep at them through the beautifully designed transparent gate. Nhial smiles and nudges Majak. "Look, do you recognize those people over there?" Majak says no. "I can't blame you. It's been long. I am seeing familiar faces. I can see Saturnino Lohure Hilangi, Majok Mac Aluong, Nyuon Bany, Malath Lueth, Arok Thon Arok, Ageer Gum, Peter Panhom Thanypiny, Francis Ngor, ...

"Brothers, let's finish the routine first," interrupts St. Paul. "We have scanned through the Book of Deeds and we found that you're all clean. Welcome to the Garden of Eden, brethren." Nhial and Majak happily walk in.

Before they reach the other crew who are eagerly waiting to hug and kiss them, St. Peter calls them back. "I'm afraid, there's a little problem. We just realized we had not considered one side of you, brothers. Weren't you members of a South Sudan's political party called the SPLM?"

They exchange glances and hesitatingly say, "y-y-y-e-e-s-s, we-we-we were."

"Well, thanks for admitting that. We're afraid, there's a little problem, brethren," says St. Peter. "Any South Sudanese who supported SPLM especially after it negotiated the independence of the country, no matter how many good deeds he did while on earth, shall never enter the Kingdom of God."

With tears rolling down their cheeks, Majak asks: "Why why why, Brother Peter? We have been very good people. We lived exemplary lives among South Sudanese. You can't do this to us."

Peter shakes his head in disagreement.

The pair kneels and pleads with the holy men. "Look, guys," narrates St. Paul, "There is nothing we can do right now rather than allowing the rule to take its course. The SPLM issue is a big deal here in Heaven. Even some angels have been assigned to solely watch the activities of the once adorable party. And I think the best way we can explain this is to remind you of one of the quotes by Desmond Tutu: 'If you are neutral in situations of injustice, you have chosen the side of the oppressor. If an elephant has its foot on the tail of a mouse and you say that you are neutral, the mouse will not appreciate your neutrality.'"

The pair lets out deafening cries.

"Guys, stop weeping. Crying won't help. Whether to enter Heaven or not is nonnegotiable," continues Peter.

"Tutu's quote explains everything. When your colleagues in the SPLM government were raping South Sudanese politically, economically and socially, you chose to keep mum. You just watched the multitude writhe in pain. The SPLM did more destruction to the citizens than the successive Khartoum regimes. SPLM killed the hopes for a better tomorrow, the very hopes that helped them survive and achieve an independent South Sudan. After the international community granted South Sudanese independence, the SPLM turned into a group of shameless liars and thieves - a mafia. Contrary to their promises they made to the public, the SPLM proved itself blind and deaf. It introduced social injustices. The former Bushmen pauperized the citizens who had counted on them during the long civil war. When it assumed power in 2005, the SPLM got involved in a number of grand malpractices. They neglected their roles and focused on self-enrichment. The poor got poorer. That's it, Brethren. No single SPLM member shall enter Heaven. It's written. Now, go to Hell. It's not far from here."

The pair had hoped that heaven was the place to be. With the breaking news delivered by the Holy Men, the pair faints. Hours later, they gain consciousness only to find themselves in front gate of a fortified town guarded by some mean-looking horned-men and women. "Hey macs, you expect to be welcomed? Where do you think this is? Heaven," Barks a Cerberus-shaped guard.

He grabs Majak and Nhial by the ears and drags them towards

the entrance of the facility. He kicks them on the butts and bangs the door.

Hell

To their amazement, the new place looks more of an earthly penitentiary, contrary to the biblical frightful descriptions of Hell. It looks awful though. It's afternoon. People are in groups. As the chaos in the new place mesmerizes them and with their mouths wide open, they hardly believe what they are seeing.

A huge crowd was mocking a small group of dark-skinned familiar men. As they get closer, they find out that it is some short man trying to stop a fight between two groups.

Unsurprisingly, these are all SPLM senior officials and members participating in a face-off with their former enemies on earth. The notable ones here are Salva Kiir, Pagan Amum, John Luk, Wani Igga, Ann Itto, Makuei Lueth, Kuol Manyang, Rizik Zachariah, Rebecca Nyandeng and many others.

Nhial approaches Barnaba Marial, and without greetings, asks him to explain what is going on.

"It's a very long story, brother. Kiir is bullied everyday as usual. Our enemies have resumed the earthly disagreements and hate here in hell. Dr. Lam Akol and a bunch of other unpatriotic South Sudanese have befriended Omar Bashir and Joseph Kony," Marial explains.

"Dr. Lam always harasses Kiir. And whenever Kiir tries to discipline him, Bashir emerges with his crewmembers, including Thabo Mbeki, Hu Jintao, Yau Yau. Yesterday, Bashir himself broke Kiir's jaws. He kicked his teeth in too. Anyway, welcome brothers. At least your presence here is of great advantage to us. We will always fight off Bashir and company."

Few weeks elapse. Majak and Nhial learn a lot. It's like many people hold grudges against the South Sudanese in Hell. Some of them who are trying to retaliate for injustices committed by South Sudanese. One such a group is that of Ugandan businessmen who got cheated in the Dura saga.

They had lodged a case at their High Court, seeking for a declaration that the refusal of the South Sudan government to pay them as per the Memorandum of Understanding with Uganda is unlawful. However, every noise they made went unheard. South Sudan turned a deaf ear. As a result, they mistreat the SPLM. SPLM members are the cooks, dishwashers, toilet cleaners and other types of odd job doers. In other words, they're living in hell within hell. To be continued....

Jesus of Nazareth

December 26, 2011

THOUGH I'M NOT YOUR FAITHFUL, I WANT TO TALK TO YOU TODAY. My friends say you're a good friend of theirs. They say good things about you. They even encouraged me to read your biography written in a book titled The New Testament.

In that book, I learned a lot about you; you performed miracles: raised the dead, fed a multitude with only two fish & five loaves of bread. You even walked on water. Wonderful.

Well, the most stunning thing I got to know about you is where you were born, in a manger! Under poor conditions. Damn! And the then ruler wanted to have you slain because he learnt you were to be great, a king, forcing your parents to flee to Egypt with you. Sadly, you lost your life to some ungrateful folks, your own people. Sorry, mate.

You know what? - We share one or two things in common; I was born in a forest, under a tall tree where there were no medicines. No food. No nothing. Worst of all, someone lied to my then president, Omar Bashir, that I would be great. So, he ordered his soldiers to make man-made rains of bombs and missiles rain on my village, causing my mother to sneak me and my siblings into Kenya.

See? We share some significant similarities though your father was a carpenter and mine, a soldier. Your mother, Mary, according the book, was a church thing. My mother, Martha, is addicted to your teachings. She spends most of her time around the church. Since I was a kid, she has been reading a big book named Kitap de Duor that I later learned it's the Thuongjang translation of your life history.

Now to the point; having danced with angels, having drunk holy wine, having eaten heavenly birthday cake and having delighted during your two-thousandth and something birthday anniversary the other day, I want you to think about my countrymen, leaders in particular. Do me a favor; just concentrate on my country's issues.

Don't even think about our neighbors. Kenyans are strong now. They hold any stubborn politician by the ear. Ugandans are super fine; they frog-march thief leaders to police stations. Forget about the people of the Democratic Republic of Congo. They're gone. Bad leadership has swallowed them alive, whole and intact. It's too late to rescue them.

North Sudanese will be okay. They just realized that Bashir's decades-long regime has been nothing but thievery plus dictatorship. The youths have been politically charged. They will topple the bhang-smoking Bashir the Gadhafi way. Wait and see. Give them few days. Though Ethiopians are practicing the word exodus, don't worry about them. You will find out what they are running away from, later on. Deal, right?

I'm from South Sudan, an African state that just attained independence from the descendants and believers of Prophet Mohamed, the founder of Islam who happens to be your religious rival. No, the word rival is more of a sport; he is your religious enemy. By the way, I was made to understand the other day that his followers are converting more people all over the world as many turn away from Christianity on grounds of failure to uphold Christian values by church leaders. I heard that big church leaders, really big ones, sleep around with young boys; some, with married women. Someone said Catholic is the worst. It's crazy.

Back to the point, my leaders liberated us from Arabs, a fact that makes them think they're untouchable, unquestionable. They're running the affairs of the nation the way that pleases them. They have customized the national wealth. They talk too much and do little or nothing at all. They invest outside the baby-nation. They have bought expensive houses in the neighboring countries; some have houses in America and Europe!

The vehicles they ride are like those of the U-S hip hop stars - highly costly. As the people they allegedly went to the bush for get consumed by acute poverty, most of them spend money, public money, on travels and unnecessary projects. I heard they recently had a retreat in Mombasa whereby they 'burnt' millions of Shillings.

Something keeps telling me that South Sudan is a polite word for corruption. Everyone talks about it; in the streets, in bars, in matatus, under trees, everywhere. Everyone speaks against it; church leaders, politicians, women, boys and girls. And nothing happens. Every new day is just like the other day. Even the president, a bearded man who always wears cowboy hat, always says he's fighting it but his efforts are ever abortive. I'm afraid, if the president doesn't do anything about corruption in his government, I think, dogs, cats and even cows will begin to complain about it!

My leaders are busy. In fact, they have been busy, busy working on personal projects and stealing. Yes, stealing. Even the anti-corruption officials who supposedly prevent corruption are involved. One of them is, this week, in the news for embezzling millions of pounds. See?

Opposition leaders who are supposed to act as check and balance of the ruling party are useless. They represent tribes. They don't have substantial agendas. They're all nothing but a bunch of sycophants. All they strive for is position. Position. Position. Position.

Civil society organizations are not any better. They are run by lazy mutes. I'm not sure if they really understand their roles. Or if they do, the fact that they get funding from the government deactivates them. They're good at keeping silent.

If you're going to do anything, please start with SSTV. Shut it down! News bulletin begins with a minister and ends with another. All they say is where they visit and when, where they will visit and when. What they plan to do. That's all. Directors work hand in hand with the government. They waste the young reporters as they instruct them what stories to chase and what not to, leaving no room for creativity, thus 'murdering' their potentials and stunting journalistic growth as well.

The news gatherers are warned against asking big men 'bad questions.' You should see them in the field. No questions asked. If any, it could be after the minister forgot to include, in his yapping, the duration of his or her visit. They shamelessly blamelessly place a minister before a camera. He then talks, talks and talks, talks about nothing. No one understands the contents of SSTV programs. They are hosted by old dudes with ancient mentality. Don't hesitate to shut it down. Please!

The riches of the newest nation are being looted by foreign nationals with the help of our leaders. Let's talk about job opportunities. Companies are mushrooming. Organizations are already in place and others are coming soon, both local and international. Instead of channeling all these opportunities to the badly needy employable youth, our rulers give them out to their friends across the borders.

This is how it goes: an influential guy orders his friend or brother in the department of immigration to process national IDs for his girlfriend, her friends and even friends of her friends. Remember, they're not South Sudanese. They are economic immigrants who escape economic crises in their countries. These guys eventually get jobs because they're highly qualified and experienced.

All this goes undetected because the labor ministry seems to be reluctant on this matter. It should have a committee that monitors the activities of NGOs. Most NGOs think South Sudanese are incapable of working, or more precisely, unemployable. This is why foreigners have taken over almost everything in Juba - public transport industry, hotels. And leaders pretend that there is nothing wrong with it. Hail Mary!

The youth are good for nothing either. I think they choose to tolerate poor governance because the leaders are their uncles and aunts who sometimes support them. Hence, making necessary noise against corrupt individuals would be like biting the fingers that feed you. There's a representative in the government. The dude is rarely seen. Nobody knows what he is up to. Perhaps he fits well in the skirts of: "If you can't beat them, join them."

In conclusion, please make them realize what they are leaders for. President Salva says his government is zero-tolerant to corruption. Make him mean it. Make him differentiate friendship from government business. I want to see him act upon any official who fails to account for his spending. Once more, make the MPs represent their constituents, not their football teams of children and concubines.

The people they go to the parliament for are pretty poor. Living standards haven't changed since your father created earth. No roads. No health centers. No running water. It's worst in my birth place, Jonglei. Insecurity tops the list of things to worry about when you get to my state. It's easier to kill someone than buy a bottle of beer in Jonglei. The issue requires a simple solution, but no one seems to long for it. Thanks to too much nose picking amongst the top leaders........! Don't tell them what I just told you lest someone shaves my dreadlocks with a broken piece of glass.

A moment of truth; I lied to you about who actually wanted to murder me. It wasn't Bashir; it was the incumbent Vice President, Riek Machar. He got deceived by some witch that I would one day be a problem to him. He ordered his soldiers to kill me. They went about killing every one of my kind in Bor but they couldn't harm me because my mum fled with me.

His soldiers drove away our cattle, about seven-hundred and fifty heads - our only means of livelihood by then. I was born to be a cattle keeper or maybe a cattle rustler. His actions changed the whole thing. I'm now counted amongst learned South Sudanese. My friends call me white collar hustler... [Smiles] Besides, I'm friends with him now. And he happens to be my favorite politician. Say hi to your Dad. Bye, my friend.

Failed State by Design

May 14, 2012

In my book, South Sudanese are deaf and the SPLM-led government is a big fat man, who, in presence of the deaf, farts so loudly with a long note - forgetting that the deaf have the sense of smell. What a man!

Though there is no universal definition of a failed state, a failed state can be a nation seen as having failed at some of the basic conditions and responsibilities of a sovereign government, according to scholars.

Whoever takes all the blames is the government which comprises of individuals in the executive, legislative and judiciary branches of the government. One of the core indicators of a failed state is extreme political corruption. Let me start it off with corruption because it is the only disease every single failure a nation suffers stems from.

Firstly, you seriously need to remember that the Government of South Sudan was granted self-autonomy in January 9, 2005 not July 9, 2011. This means it has been exercising sovereignty just like any other African governments, but with exception of few restrictions such as buying of arms and ammunitions and involvement in some international treaties.

Corruption: Corruption is one of the things most talked about in African governments but South Sudan's is the worst. A Kenyan writer, Peter Wanyonyi in his article titled South Sudan Adopted Kenya's Worst Habit published on The Standard website on March 18, 2012 writes:

"Corruption is stifling the new State, too — the South Sudanese appear to have heartily taken to heart the Kenyan tradition of kitu kidogo. Corruption is so bad that the cost of doing business in the new country is among the highest in the world. Everyone is on the take and ministers are said to ask openly for bribes to approve deals."

It's at its climax. Everyone talks about it but no one does anything about it, because, I think, nobody wants to die right now. And with the "electrical fault" burning down offices along with important documents, attempts to bring to book those involved in grand corruption will always bear no fruits.

In the beginning, out of love or sympathy or whatever it was, the international community and individual friendly countries pumped billions of dollars into the then region for development.

But little did they know that it was going to be individuated and used to enlarge few specific stomachs.

Nobody dared to make necessary noise about the stolen billions of dollars until Arthur Akuein, the former finance minister showed up the other day and tried to name and shame some leaders. How did the case go? We all believe that billions got stolen but the concerned institutions such as anti-corruption commission and judiciary just don't have the capacity to find out who the thieves are, how much they have stolen and when.

The recent court case of Pagan Amum generates more questions than answers. The weirdest thing about it was the speed with which the court ran with it - neck breaking speed, I guess. Where on this God's good earth, especially during these modern times, would a high-profile corruption case take less than a second to file a lawsuit, try the accused, and announce the verdict?! Jesus Christ! It says a lot about our judicial system.

Well, he did not "eat" the cash. Where did it go then? Who ate it? If Akuein-dit had wired it into the account of SPLM, why does it seem hard to arrive at the truth? SPLM is a well-structured political organization administered by prominent officials. Why couldn't the team investigating the scandal, if any, interrogate those that were "close" to the huge amount, the likes of the manager, finance officials and administrators?

Come on. Don't tell me the dollars flew away because I know very well that they do not have wings. Neither do they develop wings; not American dollars! Someone somewhere celebrates seven days a week for illegally owning that money. If the police, court and anti-corruption commission can't fix this simple puzzle, what exactly are they? By-standers or spectators, I believe.

I perceive the return of Akuein as a gift from God, a "John Black" those who really care about the image of South Sudan should use to whip the backs of whoever greedily swallowed the billions. Unfortunately, no one wants to own up the human whip. I believe he knows the thieves and the amount each stole but he just cannot do anything now.

He is so powerless. He has no one to run to for help. In my mind, the whole saga is a chess game. The black queen is in a position to attack and capture a white rook but it just can't do it because the rook is lying within the L-shape of a white knight which happens to be covering its comrade.

If, by whatever reason, the black queen decides to capture the rook, the knight would react by attacking and capturing the queen. It's a deadlock. I can't say who the chess pieces symbolize. It is up to you to put it together.

In international law, one must have tangible evidence to accuse a corrupt individual government official. Failure to do that may cost you a jail term. This makes it impossible to fight corruption all over the world, particularly in South Sudan. But in real sense, corruption is seen through many things in so many ways. Check this out: A senior polygamous government employee X got appointed in 2005. He has so many kids such that he never remembers their names each time he visits them:

"Hey you. Come here my daughter. Remind me of your name. Who is your mother? I promised I will never forget your name again," he once fumbled.

He gets Y salary per month. He owns posh houses in Nairobi and Kampala. He also possesses a fleet of expensive rides; even his house attendants commonly called "aunties" ride his old V-8s. He is handling school fees for both his Arsenal FC of children and a Man U of nieces and nephews and in-laws. High-class living is what they have indulged in. Children do eat out. Pizza Inn is their dining table. He has bought a number of plots in Juba. Now do the Maths. An X salary times seventy-seven months is equal to......? Now, add up his overall spending and subtract it from the 77-month salary. I bet you would arrive at negative something if you're a good mathematician.

Anti-Corruption Commission

Since its inception in 2006, the commission has never prosecuted any single official for involvement in corrupt deals. In fact, it has never publicly named one even though it was investigating about sixty cases of corruption. The commission, normally animalized as a dog, does not bark; leave alone the fact that it is toothless. Why is it that weak and useless? Someone would say it is simply because one cannot investigate a fellow thief. It is like, after carrying out a bank robbery with your pal, you knock at his door the following day and question why he robbed the bank. It's just weird and silly. It never happens! As you read this sentence, South Sudan Law Society is staying in the ass of one of the anti-corruption senior officials for embezzling millions. How do you expect such a person to face another embezzler?

Members of Parliament, National Assembly:

Shortly before or after declaration of independence, some great news echoed that Obama administration handed to Kiir, a list containing names of 13 top government officials believed to be behind the reason why South Sudan refused to develop since they stole and stashed billion dollars in foreign banks. Rumors said Obama wanted the 13 out of the first country's cabinet.

The MPs, our MPs first boldly, rationally and constitutionally demanded that Kiir reveal the 13 economic vampires before they approve the cabinet. But surprisingly, the boldness, rationale and constitutional obligations melted away, giving the cabinet a green light. Reports say the SPLM members; the huge majority in the parliament neutralized the efforts to have Kiir publicize the names. For Christ's sake, why did they throw in the towel yet it was and still is a national grave matter? Every citizen wanted to know who the 13 are.

This leaves a simple normal-minded citizen like me to contemplate, freestyle in thinking. Here I go: Note the word "top" that appears a number of times in the following sentences. The government is led by top SPLM members. Majority of top ministers in the government are SPLM members and the top party in the parliament is SPLM that raise top votes. More importantly, amongst the Obama list are top government officials. I think an element of "top" influenced the move by the parliament to not bug Kiir with the Obama list. I love my MP!

Lastly, a common man may not know the ugly games the government plays, the personalized decisions it makes, but he is always at the receiving end. In so many ways, he pays for all the wrongdoings the government commits; selfishness, political unproductiveness.

I know South Sudan has changed a lot compared to the state it was in 2005 but what, in developmental terms, can the government brag about? After seven years, roads, modern roads, are still struggling to "get out" of Juba.

Clean drinking water is a problem. Only few selected homes in the city get running water. The whole city depends on Ethiopians for their tank water. It's comical. The USAID-sponsored water project at Hamza Inn was meant for the citizens. Contrarily, foreigners run it. They sell water to its owners. Hospitals and clinics are useless.

Nurses are ever grumbling over arrears. Recently, two children died at Juba's Sabah hospital simply because no doctor attended to them. Besides, importers bring in drugs that expired ten years ago. The same with many other trade items; how do they get in? Someone told me that a customs officer, to check out goods quality, say milk, removes a packet and drinks it up. If nothing happens to him in ten minutes, he nods his head in acceptance, allowing the importer to enter with the goods. God help us!

Don't you think it's the reason why a medic at Juba hospital complained the other day? This dude said the number of corpses overwhelms the mortuary. The numbers increase day by day. There are no enough rooms to store them before they are taken for burial. Why are South Sudanese dying like flies? What is killing them? Expired items, I believe.

Good citizens are getting wasted at petrol stations. They painfully spend hours on long queues as they hustle to buy fuel at Somali-owned gas stations. Foreigners have monopolized fuel business. They hoard it and sell it at any time they want, and at any price. If we cannot control what is rightfully ours, aren't we losers?

Life is pathetic. Pound is depreciating hour after hour. $100 is now equivalent to 500 SP. What the heck? The rate is being controlled by cattle keepers. Isn't it funny? What's the central bank doing? Nothing! Living cost is so high. People are suffering. Food prices have tripled within few months of independence. There is no food. The little has been bought up by the haves. People are hungry.

A state does not have to be forty years old in order to be considered a failed state and vice versa; it depends on every step the government makes and its impact on the lives of citizens. Believe it or not, the world knows that South Sudan is a failed state but it just can't let it out because it would paint a bad image on splitting of countries.

It would discourage the international community from supporting a marginalized people who would want to be a separate nation. The foreign institutions can fool people but not everyone. They are business entities, remember. You can't expect them to admit their failures, publicly. Think! I strongly believe that the percentage of those living below poverty line will shoot up soon. No, it has already shot up.

Think on Your Feet

April 24, 2019

Dear Dr. Riek, you should now begin to think on your feet. Look. President Salva Kiir, for whatever reason, can have your throat slit in Juba in broad daylight, with or without security arrangements in place.

After all, Kiir, the leader, barely follows rules. He has sullied the transitional constitution a billion times. And you know it.

Having said that, Kiir appears to have finally agreed, from the bottom of his heart, to tolerate, to accommodate you this time round.

With all the academic wealth and political experience you have acquired over the years, you always annoyingly remain unable to think clearly and quickly when important matters arise.

And this is when Kiir seizes the opportunity to outmaneuver you. Using Sun Tzu philosophy, Kiir defeated you twice – in 2013 and 2016. And by the look of things, the third defeat is imminent.

During the first incident, the presidential guards practiced Tzu's 'When you surround an army, leave an outlet free. Do not press a desperate foe too hard' on you. They knew your residence. They could have killed you if they really wanted to.

What they did was scare you out of Juba and as calculated, you started making war statements upon finding and gathering your soldiers in the Upper Nile Region.

In 2016, you failed to see the importance of staying with Kiir at the palace in order to collectively order your commanders to stand down. After indecisively arriving at your residence at the foot of Jebel Kujur, the 5-million-dollar-motivated Gen. King Paul chased you to DR Congo, according to Ateny Wek, the presidential press secretary.

Now, you're about to be checkmated by President Kiir, again. He has publicly appealed to you to come back to set up the new interim government despite being behind schedule. He argues that those provisions will be actualized as you work together, with time – a request you have turned down.

Let's be realistic. Three years ago, you had a protection unit, comprising of soldiers who were just as angry and tribally motivated as the presidential guards. What happened? Like dogs, they attacked each other, causing you to run for your life.

So, how would a "well-trained, unified, and cantoned army" help you given the fact that the soldiers will still be made up of men from your communities (Dinka and Nuer) – soldiers that are loyal to their ethnic groups, not their nation?

Sir, insistence on implementation of every activity of the pre-transitional period is a waste of time. You're just being egoistic and hardheaded - traits that are sending wrong signals to the whole world. Just come back home.

Tread Carefully, Michael-dit

May 29, 2014

WHILE YOU EXECUTE YOUR DUTIES AS THE NATIONAL MINISTER OF information and broadcasting, and the official spokesperson of the government of South Sudan, you're making two grave mistakes.

One, you're becoming a stigmata on the reputation of Bor community. And two, you're doing yourself a great harm – digging your own grave.

I will not dwell much on the fact that you and some of your peers are, in so many ways, tainting the already 'vandalized' face of Bor. We will talk about that some other day.

Uncle Makuei, do you know your leadership net worth? Do you know how much you weigh on the political scale? In case you didn't know, you mean a lot, Uncle. You're a great man. You're a freedom fighter, a liberator. You are a senior government official, a minister.

You're one of the members of parliament representing Bor people in the national legislative assembly.

Your contributions in attaining and bettering South Sudan are inestimable.

Again, you're one of the highly educated Bor elders. You're an idol in the eyes of Bor people; they celebrate you. Musicians have composed songs about you. They sing your name.

All those spectacular achievements that put you in a critical position whereby you have to watch what you say. You represent. That means anything that flies out of your mouth can either kill or save lives. It can either heighten or lessen tensions, perhaps violence.

So, why are you everywhere falsely accusing everyone of rebellion? What happened to political correctness? What happened to diplomacy? A rebel is a person who takes part in an armed rebellion against the constituted authority, especially in the hope of improving conditions.

Uncle Makuei, these are modern times. The whole world is watching every move each and every South Sudan's leader makes. You don't have to personally pick an EX-34 Chain gun and shoot down a whole village in order to be indicted.

This is 2014. This is digital age. Anything dangerous one wishes, thinks or does is recorded and used against him or her in future.

There is something called hate speech. A hate speech maker can be defined as any person who utters words intended to incite feelings of contempt, hatred, hostility, violence or discrimination against any person, group or community on the basis of ethnicity or race.

In your book, media houses are rebels. Church leaders are rebels. Innocent displaced bereaved hungry women are rebels. Even malnourished dying babies are rebels! What sense does that make? What happened to morality?

I think many could categorize most of your statements under hate speech. You cannot refer to a baby a rebel just because it hails from a particular community whose some members have staged an insurgency.

You and your comrades can say anything about anyone, about any community, anytime, with impunity. That's okay *inu* you rule. But for me, I call it short-term impunity *inu* there comes a time when one has to account for everything he had said or done or not done during his heydays.

Don't ever think that you're untouchable, forever. None of your colleagues are, either; including your boss, Kiir Mayardit.

Hate speech might not have been constituted in the South Sudan interim constitution. But it is constituted under international law. Worse the powers you think you have do not exist in the global village.

I often hear members of the ruling clique cheering you on as you 'defend' the government. I hear them clapping their hands every time you come on TV to speak against the West.

I read Facebook and Twitter posts by your 'supporters' in which they pat you on the shoulder, encouraging you to keep 'defending' the legitimate government. Cool.

However, Uncle, what you don't know or negligent about is that, when that day comes, Salva Kiir will not be there for you, Buor will not be able to protect you, your colleagues will giggle and some will, in fact, throw parties to celebrate your descend.

I'm not telling you to stop supporting your regime, Uncle. I am not telling you to join Dr Riek, to be a rebel. Nor am I asking you to resign. No.

What I am trying to say is that, carry on with your work but tread carefully. Your mouth. Your tongue. Your lips. I repeat: t-r-e-a-d c-a-r-e-f-u-l-l-y.

Summarily, in your quest for cleansing the skunk-stinky face of the Government of the Republic of South Sudan, do not be like a man who takes off the only clothes he possesses to clothe another naked man.

Kerbino Wol vs Ber Mor Ben

June 18, 2020

"Get up. Grab this gun. Get up. Follow me!" My cousin interrupts my siesta. I just arrived at our birthplace Malual Chaat for the first visit. It is my day two here, spending time chatting with relatives, especially the elderly, who are telling me stories about life in the area since Kerbino Kuanyin Bol started the liberation struggle there in 1983.

So, when Gai Arou yells orders at me, I am sleeping under a huge tamarind tree. "Take this shotgun," he insists. I get scared, though. "What are we going to kill, man?" I ask. "Is it a gazelle or lion? And by the way, I don't even know how to use guns."

But his voice tinges with finality: "Do not worry but just follow me." He moves faster. I struggle to keep up with him as the narrow footpath keeps meandering among bushes and tall savannah grass. Within minutes, we bounce onto a group of equally armed youth, under a tree. They have been waiting for us.

They comprise of youth mostly from various clans in Kolnyang. I can tell because each representative says his name, his clan and the number of youth he brought along. So, there are Abeng, Guelei, Abie and Adool. There are also Paleek, Deer, Kuoi and Ateet. In total, we are about fifty Ber Mor Bens.

One of the youth steps forward to address us. I don't catch his name, though. But he tells us that we, the area youth, have been requested by the army to catch, dead or alive, a young rebel, who is running towards the area – that he "is a very dangerous man the West has offered money to overrun J1".

"The soldiers at the barrack do not know our savannah terrain and because it's rainy season, their vehicles are, of course, useless. The jeeps can't move an inch at all," says the young man. He is short, muscular, and in war fatigue like John Rambo. He has two missing upper teeth, not to mention the lower teeth that must have been removed during initiation.

Off we march in single file. The fastest guys run toward different directions, probably as part of reconnaissance mission. We move slowly but carefully, with some keeping their eyes up on the trees and others searching for footprints on the wet ground.

Two hours fly by and there is still no sign of the hunted. My feet hurt. I'm dehydrating. I'm starving. And the gun is getting heavier. I'm thinking of throwing it away and wandering the kcuf back to Malual Chaat, however, so many dangers - including lions, leopards and lone heartless tribesmen I have heard of, cross my mind. Thus, I soldier on.

My cousin Gai, who has me next to him throughout is starting to worry about me. I can see regret in his eyes. He keeps looking at me with the corner of his eye. "Why did I bring this city guy here? What was I really thinking," says Gai, under his breath.

Suddenly, we see the tall grass moving from afar, forcing us to kneel military style, ready to light up whatever it is. I hear everyone cock his gun. I try mine but that thing is harder than I think. It almost breaks my soft thumb. "Xe xen weke," shouts a voice. It's one of the recon boys. Sigh!

He says he just saw at least two people seated under a tree. "They looked huge and in civilian town clothes. They must be the ones," he convinces us. Side by side, off we run towards the direction he pointed at. My wrist watch reads 5:12pm.

About 20 or so minutes later, I slow down to take a pee. As I look for a tree trunk to hide my weewee pipe, guns suddenly go off: brrrrrrttttttotototot. Brrrrttttotototot. Brrrtttttttotototot. AK-47s and G3 rule the air. I use the trunk I wanted to pee on as my cover.

I try to shoot but I can't see the target. I am a step behind too. So, I chill. I can hear bullets "pew pew pew" above me. One misses me by whiskers.

After some minutes, probably five, firing from the other end stops. I think the bad guys are outnumbered and outgunned, forcing them to throw away their guns and start running for their lives. As a result, the hardcore Ber Mor Bens stop shooting and start chasing them.

In the nick of time, they are caught. When I arrive at the scene. I see a well-built man that looks familiar. I move closer. "Kerbino!" I shout. "So it's you? What did you do in Juba, man?" Seated between his two comrades, on the wet green grass, he just stares at me as he breathes heavily. He is visibly fatigued after the chase.

"Oh. Ye wek wetke Buor?" He asks. "Rasta, what are you doing here too? By the way, did I kill anyone in the crossfire? Anyway, you guys better kill me right now right here, for I'm not going back to Juba. Shoot me in the head."

And before we know it, some soldiers join us. They have been following our foot trails, and guided by the sound of gunshots. I'm surprised to see my other cousin Akim Garang Ngang. He is the most senior army officer leading the platoon.

Akim begins to speak:

"Kerbino is our brother. We all know how he ended up in the bush. But I'm not going to delve into what transpired in Juba, from the time he was thrown in, tried and pardoned. He's a good young man, someone whose contributions to the nation are tangible. Yes, he declared insurgency, but are we the ones to end his life? How many people, very useless people, have rebelled against the Juba regime, yet are still alive and holding big positions in the government – some even dine with the President today? Secondly, if he has to die, he has to die somewhere else, not in Bor. We must not allow our good name and good soil to be soiled by his blood. I'm not saying he's innocent nor am I saying he's guilty. We just do not know what's happening in Juba anymore."

Akim tells us to let what happened in the Bor Jungle today remain in Bor jungle. He takes three guns off Ber Mor Bens and handed them to Kerbino and his comrades and instructs five herders to guide the men out of Bor land, towards Lafon.

"Please, Kerbino, these boys will lead you to safety, to Eastern Equatoria where you will find your way out of the country – Uganda or Kenya – if you wish," he continues. "On what to subsist on on the way, worry not, for there are game throughout these side of the country. Kill them for food."

He also gives Kerbino full clips to use to hunt animals and

protect themselves. "Rasta," Kerbino calls out, referring to me. "I will contact you on Facebook when I make it out alive....and please write down all the names of these men and keep the list with you..."

"Ding dong ding dong," my doorbell rang, waking me up. So, it was a dream? Nooo!

Eat First, Die First – Sorry

April 8, 2020

ABOUT THREE YEARS AGO, WHEN THE SOUTH SUDAN ECONOMY WAS IN really bad shape and hunger biting harder, a senior military officer died in what appeared to be a foodborne outbreak in Western Bahr el Ghazal State.

About 60 soldiers, who were participating in a UN-facilitated workshop, ate some food at a hotel there. All of them were hospitalized, but their boss died shortly upon arrival at a hospital. A private died a day or so later. But the 58 soldiers made it out of the hospital alive.

The boss kicked the bucket, according to officials, because he was the first to fill his stomach with the supposedly delicious meal.

He ate the 'top layer' which happened to be laced with poison. The incident took place at Grinti, Wau, on 3 August 2017.

Had the officer humbled himself and chosen to eat together with his juniors, they might have all shared the poison – taken in small quantities of the substance, hospitalized together, and discharged together. Unfortunately, it didn't happen. RIP, colonel.

All this could be attributed to the SPLM leadership style of eating before everyone else. As a child, I witnessed this hollow leadership. My sister Abech, mum and I visited dad in Narus, Eastern Equatoria, in 1990, I think.

There, we met another kid named Ayen, whom I have apologetically forgotten both face and father's name. The other thing I remember about her is somebody named Makuach Ajot; probably her uncle.

Anyway, I believe we were the only (Dinka) kids there. We would run around the small army base all day, playing and making fun of Matha (Toposa) female attires – the animal skin skirts.

I recollect always seeing soldiers preparing meals and serving the fat jovial men playing cards and dominoes in tree shades by a seasonal river before they would sit on empty oil gallons to scramble for few bones left.

This was so interesting and surprising to me, because my mums (Teresa and Akuany), who always prepared meals at home, ate last. We, the children, were always the first to eat.

21 years later, the SPLM leaders achieved independence. They assumed power. Old habits die hard, White people often say. Unsurprisingly and with their mouths wide open, they marched to Juba, the power base, with their eat-first bush mentality.

And boom! they dived into the river of power and petrodollars, forgetting to - with the help of billions of dollars - open up and macadamize road networks, build state-of-art health facilities, bring piped water, electrify towns, protect the common man, encourage agriculture, recruit the finest brains, and many more.

Worst of all, they left their own soldiers who protect(ed) them to die slowly - little pay-, salary delay-, poor feeding-, poor health-, and hopelessness-induced deaths.

From Nimule to Renk and Tambura to Pibor, soldiers live like beggars while their bosses live kingly in Juba. No. Ninety percent of soldiers are actually debatably beggars right now. You should see some of them try to "rob beg" motorists along Yei Rd in Juba.

Just like locusts completely strip the foliage and stems of plants, the former guerilla fighters plundered (plunder) the wealth of the nation. They looted and are still looting everything there is to loot – land, gold, oil proceeds, country's future, name it. They are even now selling crude oil in advance.

The SPLM men and women grew greedier - triggering the 5-year civil war, which resulted in nearly 400,000 deaths, displacement in millions, and maimed economy.

However, they didn't know how Mama Nature operates. They never knew times like these would come – an era when every government must tackle Covid-19 with whatever health facilities and expertise they have at hand. Ian Bremmer calls it G-Zero World in his 2012 book: Every Nation for Itself.

Now all borders have been locked – nobody in nobody out - and flights have been suspended in order to contain the pandemic. Every nation must 'unleash' its finest doctors to treat finest leaders.

And the twist is, coronavirus doesn't play with anyone, especially older people, who have pre-existing health conditions such as diabetes, HIV/AIDS and heart problems. South Sudanese ancestors forbid, but when the virus hits Junub, the first to eat will be the first to die. Sorry.

Protest Not

May 10, 2019

THOUGH I'VE BEEN SICK AND TIRED OF THE KIIR ADMINISTRATION'S unending impuissance, leadership bankruptcy, lack of political ideologies and will to run the country as expected, and sincerely wouldn't mind if anyone or group superseded J1 and subsequently threw into dungeons or "Zan zans" Kiir and his cohorts, I'm not in support of the alleged mass protests scheduled to take place in Juba and other major towns on or before May 16.

This is because it isn't worth it for now. It's not worth it because it's not an original idea; you must have borrowed it from the people of the Sudan who recently ousted their longtime potentate, Omar al-Bashir.

After decades of suppression and impoverishment, the Sudanese united against their common enemy, al-Bashir, and demanded for his resignation. After months of being called a bluff, they intensified the peaceful protests, forcing the ruler to step down.

South Sudanese are not Sudanese. Nor are they Algerians. Seventy-three percent of South Sudanese are illiterate, according to UNESCO. This means people in this country do not know their economic, social, and political rights. Hence, given that such alarming level of ignorance, it is certain South Sudanese will not join the protests. They will side with their respective tribal leaders, who often use them for their own selfish gains.

"A hungry man can't see right or wrong. He just sees food," wrote Pearl S Buck, American writer and novelist. If you want to control a people, starve them. Reduce them to paupers. When they become malnourished, they will be thinking about nothing but food. And you become their king. This is what is happening right now.

I feel you the organizers of the protests. But this noble cause is likely to be met with counter-demonstrations, especially by the hounds whose uncles and aunts will shoo unto you. With the volatility of the current situation, this might turn violent and subsequently brutal as it gets tribal. And the elites you intend to depose will just smile and sip cold wine in their places.

I get it. You mean well. It's a constitutional right to protest. You want change, for better. You'd like the people to enjoy the benefits of the hard-earned independence. However, the ones who will counter your protests are probably those that are suffering in the hands of the regime.

Another factor to consider is the kind of government you want to write placards for, to protest against. The SPLM-led government is recovering from the bush mentality. It's uncouth, barbarous, dictatorial, and kleptocratic. It's devoid of ideas that can UAE-lize or Rwanda-ize South Sudan.

After all, one reasons with a government that reasons. In other parts of the world, governments equip riot police with necessary tools such as shields, shin guards, batons, crowd management spray and teargas to quell protests. Here, security personnel are uncivilized, brute and gonzo.

In short, what I'm trying to tell you is that, you cannot liberate the "unliberatable". Wait until the people are ready for liberation, the second liberation.

This Thing

June 22, 2017

FOR YEARS NOW, THERE'S SOMETHING THAT HAS BEEN WORKING DAY and night to take apart the once united people of Lower Nadus, a country located somewhere in what the West calls the dark continent. Describing it as a Satan would be an understatement. Thus, let's just call it 'This thing'.

Even though you and I bear the brunt of its blood-sustained empire and should actually actualize the phrase enough-is-enough, we all have unfathomably allowed it to unabatedly plunder, with impunity, the riches of our collectively hard-earned land. It has been abusing our political, economic and civil rights as a people.

It has robbed us of lives, dignity, and possessions. This thing has made us the laughing stock of the world, once again. Faces of our starving half-dead children and elderly people are flashed on television screen worldwide, once again. Our neighbors maliciously smile at us, once again.

This thing is systematically ridding the country of each and everyone of us. It's feeding on the people. It started its evil program way back shortly after assuming the throne in the year 5002. After it failed to destroy Nibunuj as a whole, it wittingly resorted to the one-by-one approach, something more of the analogy of the black, white, and red bulls.

First, it attacked the Reun people. This began in the year 4102. The attacks were characterized by attack on villages, indiscriminate killing, rape and the ensuing grand displacement of hundreds of thousands of civilians who either crossed over to neighboring countries or sought safety in the UN zoos where they are 'visited' by people of the first world. They are wild animals, aren't they?

Next on its list was Ollohc people. Just like the Reun, they were humiliated and vanished from their homes. The actions of this thing turned their homeland into a Golgotha. The few who managed to flee to islands got into more trouble. The only humanitarian route was willfully blocked to starve the people to death. From the pan to the fire, isn't it?

Meanwhile, in the capital, Ubaj, salient members of Rob people were hunted down like wild animals; many were chased and gunned down in broad daylight for fun; some shot dead at pointblank and their deaths announced as mistaken identity; and others killed in cold-blood in their homes at night and shamelessly categorized under suicide cases by the establishment.

Then came Airotauqe people's turn in the year 6102. As this thing chased a giant rat through their land, the Irab speaking people suffered unimaginable suffering – killings, pillage, rape, and displacements. Farmlands and homes were set ablaze as a punishment for allegedly hosting the rodent, which this thing ironically aided its escape in Abuj. Like locusts, the forces of this thing invaded major areas such as Iey Town, Oibmay, Oborom, Idiram, name it.

And the peaceful linear settlements in Idam land, along the major road, are no more; their neighboring Kojap too. Homes and farms were scorched. This came after the indigenes were accused of harboring disciples of the rat. In the recent attacks, civilians were burnt alive.

Now in the year 7102, it's the turn of the Liewa people to face the music. The once protectors of the thing have been condemned to arbitrary arrests and detentions for sharing a birthplace with the latest enemy of the thing, a hotheaded-but-intrepid ex-military leader. So far, good young men are being kept in security facilities.

Sadly enough, though, the strong few, the ones who have what it takes to stop this monstrous bloodsucking insatiable thing from preying on its next victim, are busy minding their businesses. Some of them are partaking in human blood meals.

The Self-eating State

April 7, 2017

SOME ANIMALS EAT THEMSELVES (TO DEATH) WHENEVER THEY'RE stressed, according to zoologists. They call it self-cannibalism. It's also more of a suicide. Such a stress is caused by several factors, including poor or inadequate diet, physical pain, and extreme temperatures.

Dogs, horses, snakes, octopi, goats, and cats - zoologists say - are some of the animals that practice self-eating and suicide. From a high point such as bridge, dogs leap to their deaths; rat snakes create a circle as they eat their own tails; octopi eat up their own arms; horses eat themselves into coma or death. Just to mention but a few.

Salva Kiir's South Sudan could be likened to one of the self-eating animals, probably a dog, rat snake, or octopus. To animalize it, loosely, the Kiir Administration is the head. The body consists of the people; while abdomen is the territory.

Due to the self-inflicted pain – war and economic and humanitarian crises – and SPLM's political philosophy deficiency, the state is now eating itself to death, in so many ways:

One: The government is killing its own citizens (soldiers) on the battlegrounds, both SPLA and anti-Juba armed forces. Thousands of civilians have been killed in crossfires. Who will defend South Sudan territory in case it comes under attack by a foreign enemy? This conflict has displaced millions that are now either 'prisoners' at UN POCs or 'international beggars' at refugee camps in the neighboring countries.

Two: It's engaged in a probable genocidal act by knowingly or unknowingly preventing food aid from reaching the areas UN agencies and humanitarian groups have already declared famine-hit. Besides, Kiir-Riek violence-free peripheral areas, mostly in greater Aweil, Yambio, and Kapoeta, have witnessed starvation-related deaths due to the protraction of the unnecessary war.

Three: Misplaced priorities. The unending buying of arms and ammunition instead of food for the vulnerable people, estimated at 5 million, is undoubtedly a calculated ignorance.

Four: Habitual late payment of government staff salaries aka peanuts. The government has nearly a million employees on its payroll. These include teachers, lecturers, health workers, law practitioners, and those in the security sector. Getting the low pay after 3 months is an unimaginable suffering given the uncontrollable hyperinflation.

As a result, members of the army have resorted to the power of the gun by looting civilian property. Some extort money from road users. Others beg for food. On the other hand, the non-military employees are suffering in dignity- and impuissance-inspired silence. An employer whose workers constantly stay hungry cannot be differentiated from Beelzebub.

Five: The government, which is supposedly responsible for about 12 million citizens, is devoid of key attributes such as transparency and accountability, and sense of responsibility. It doesn't know what the people want – protection. With security, comes everything else.

Six: After pocketing billions of dollars from oil proceeds and financial aid, the government has now decided to hike taxes and introduce new and strange ones such as "Departure" tax - $20, an amount equivalent to salaries of six soldiers.

And lastly: Illiteracy, sycophancy, 'our-turnism', and us-versus-them politics have blinded the people. They cannot see who their real enemy is.

In sum, American Inventor Charles Kettering once said that "A problem well-stated is a problem half-solved." South Sudanese of all walks of life and the international community have described, with vividity and lucidity, the South Sudan problem for years. Therefore, the quicker the Kiir administration ceases dilly-dallying the better.

Leaders by Force

March 29, 2017

DEAR PAANLUEL WEL, I'VE BEEN WONDERING WHETHER GOVERNMENT officials think about what the people think about them. We're talking political and social recognition here. Reputation too.

Given what's happening in this country, don't you think every government official should explain, verbally or in writing, why he or she is an important person in the society and be recognized and treated respectfully by every common man like myself?

Title aside. Personal achievements during the 21-year struggle aside. Military ranks aside. Social status aside. Belly size aside.

Yes; every single official deserves respect, but the problem is, respect is like salary. It's earned. Isn't it? One has to work hard for it, sweat for it. If you don't work, you don't get paid. Right?

Every single appointment President Salva Kiir makes has an explanation for it. It's either the appointee is a bush-comrade, relative, friend, or just a "silencer" - an individual appointed in the name of appeasement for a certain elite or community that poses a threat to the Presidency in one way or the other.

Contrarily, in the other part of the world, those a Head of State nominates are subjected to a serious scrutiny. They are vetted. This is meant to prevent the morally corrupt from running public affairs.

"This is South Sudan, Muony," you would remind me. "Whatever makes one get a position in this country is none of anyone else's business."

OK. I presume this is because the establishment, in general, doesn't value my view, as a common man. And imagine these are matters that actually directly affect me and my fellow underdogs, the 'gunless' lot. Am I wrong?

Anyway, what a public office post holder does is what matters to me. That's my problem. It's always been and it shall always be. Depending on performance, he or she either earns contempt or my respect and recognition.

For example, a public servant that has been in the government since 2005. He's held various ministerial positions but has nothing to show for all these. He could be a good husband, a good father. He puts his family first. That's cool.

But, remember respect is a two-way traffic. You respect me and I respect you back. A leader should show me such a respect by doing what he or she was tasked to do by the President. As expected, they should build roads, electrify towns, provide running water, provide security, and I'll venerate him, praise him because I benefit from it as a layman, and I, in turn, respect him. It's business. Wele kef?

However, as you read this, some of the leaders have failed to manage their office affairs, let alone services delivery to the people.

Simple basic amenities such as toilets are faulty. That's why you see those gas-guzzlers piloted on the narrow Juba roads. The unsuspecting members of public think that the big man being chauffeured is attending an important official meeting somewhere. *Wapi?*

No. They've got it wrong. Some of the big dogs are piloted to hotels to do nothing but take the call of nature. This is because their office toilets are messed up. No running water to flush down excretions. No toilet rolls. And they can't do anything about that!

So, why in the name of God would an arrogant CDF-eating, office-abusing, indolent official expect me to recognize him by edging out of the way for him when he hasn't done nothing for me?

I believe Hegel would describe this politics they are forcing down our throats as *kampf um anerkennung*. Don't you think so?

But what has an official done to expect my respect and recognition? Why would someone who misrecognizes or unrecognizes me expect me to recognize him?

Ruweng

February 14, 2020

Dear Ruweng people, whether you like it or not, the controversy over 32 states is about Dinka versus the 63 tribes and I understand Ruweng is one of the major reasons why the Kiir administration is too adamant to let go of the 32 states. However, Dinka extremists and politicians are using it for their own selfish interests, not for you.

It's all about oil beneath your land. And it's not about you as Dinka people (Abiem-nhom and Pan e Riang) that the "Dinka government" of Kiir Mayardit would want to maintain your state for. No, brothers and sisters. It's about what you have, the oil, which makes it look like the "Dinka government" cares about you – that it holds you dear to its heart as a people. Nope.

Major oil wells - including Panthou (Heglig), Toma South, and Tor - which make up about 80 percent of the total monthly oil production - are in the Ruweng State, according to reports.

The same "Dinka government" has been drilling oil there for years, but no one but few state sons and daughters have benefited from the oil proceeds, while the ordinary people there suffer oil pollution.

Both local and international media and environmental campaign groups have been highlighting the adverse effects of irresponsible oil production there.

The residents have been witnessing birth defects – with some babies born without eyes, others without limps. Women are unable to conceive and some of those who manage to get pregnant miscarry. And adults and livestock are dying of strange diseases. As well, indigenous residents can't farm no more since their soil has been polluted. That said, allotting you, the Ruweng people, your own state will not automatically reverse the situation you are facing, for the insatiable Juba-based men and women will continue to build their economic empires at your expense.

If it's about pride, ask residents of states that are nearly or 100% Dinka. Nothing changed, my brothers. There's nothing special about having your own state. Tonj people are still slaughtering themselves and so are those in Gogrial. Gok and Western Lakes too. Jonglei still loses lives, children, and livestock to criminals.

In my opinion, you should renounce your state for the sake of the greater good of the country. In the name of peace for all, please have Kiir, Makuei and Elia revoke the 32 states.

Anyway, you are a sacrificial lamb either way. You either offer your neck to Kiir and his boys in order to win the political chess championship against Dr. Riek Machar or you choose 10 states + AAA, be part of Unity State again. You have been living among the Nuer for time immemorial, anyway.

By giving up your state, you defuse the tension or prevent a potential return to civil war. By doing so, you allow the peace parties to establish the coalition government. Peace then returns and everyone enjoys it. A Madi farmer returns to his field. The economy stabilizes. And the country prospers.

But more importantly, I'd strongly encourage your lawyers, leaders, members of parliament and Ruweng activists like Santino Ayuel Longar plus the Nuer community counterparts there to use the Petroleum Act 2012 to hold the government and the oil companies to account. With monthly 2% oil share, you could erect twin cities within a very short period of time.

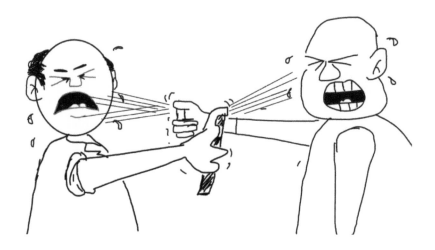

Democratize South Sudan: Tear Down the Ruling Party

August 10, 2012

FOR DEMOCRACY, THE REAL DEMOCRACY—D-E-M-O-C-R-A-C-Y—NOT just the written, sung or spoken democracy that frequently flies out of our politicians' mouths, to be realized, enjoyed, seen, smelled, tasted, felt, drunk or even eaten by all the people of the Republic of South Sudan, including the mute, deaf, amputees, blind and the one-eyed, the Sudan People's Liberation Movement's top leaders must be incited against each other.

A seed of discord must be sown amongst them now and quickly. Confuse them; Make them poke out each other's eyes! Let a rain of political teargas canisters rain on their Headquarters at

Juba's Thongpiny area. With watery and itchy eyes, let them grasp for fresh air. Like what little boys do in preparation for a fight, make them roll up their pants and sleeves to break each other's jaw politically.

In a plain language, our educated uncles and aunts describe Democracy as a regime where the rule is determined by the people. A democratic government is a government for the People by the People and of the people, meaning that the people run the government and the government is made to protect the people. Now be sincere to yourself and your country, does South Sudan fit in the above description? Is the government democratic?

On this planet earth, every child is born into some screwed up group and it is up to him or her to fight his or her way out of it or remain loyal, depending on the mindset and level of intellectuality, both natural and academic or even the borrowed brains, he or she attained during his or her transition from childhood to adulthood.

With my father being a member of SPLM/A Battalion 105 aka Ashara-kamsa or Koriom, and my mother pregnant with me during the civil war in the late eighties, I was automatically born into the SPLM. That means I am an SPLM by birth.

And since none of the opposition parties has what it takes to win my admiration, and as a good citizen, I have only two things to do and they are, one, to remain in the SPLM and two, to fight it from within. And here goes my bullet.

Let me begin with the word that I loathe the most – sycophancy, a word beautifully tattooed on many faces in the country. You need an extra eye to see the tattoo though. A sycophant is a servile self-seeker who attempts to win favor by flattering influential people.

That's it. The ruling SPLM party is a sycophant-fortified city. Back in the day, in the bush, sycophancy was a necessity. It was an air, a ticket for survival. This was because the movement's leadership was debatably tyrannical, militaristic, and vampiric. It had no time to play with dissidents. It was zero-tolerant to criticism.

Those who dared object to any decision made by the Late John Garang and seconded by his loyalists were frowned at and frog-marched to frog-ponds for punitive drowning. Some rot in dungeons. On the battle grounds, hardliners were 'shot in the back of their heads' after they compulsorily led their respective infantries to frontlines. You can put that together.

The SPLM members who are actually the liberators, the ruling elite or even the gods of life are suffering from two diseases, chronic ones: highly exaggerated sycophancy and empty loyalty. These two diseases are viral and hereditary and the root cause of the irresoluteness in the government, the very reason it is weak-kneed. Being loyal is not bad. But the saddest part of it is that SPLM loyalists got addicted to their role until they morphed into sycophants.

Inarguably, the country is in the pocket of a cultish group of the much-hyped influential figures, namely: Salva Kiir, Riek Machar, Wani Igga, Pagan Amum, Kuol Manyang, Rebecca Nyandeng, Hoth Mai, Gier Chuang plus some underpublicized souls, most of whom are wealthy businesspeople.

They are all SPLM. What they agree on is final, regardless of its potential impact on the common man. What they do, or fail to do, unveils their real faces. It indicates the exactitude of their unspoken intentions – to rid the country of the poor, which make up to 70 percent of the total population. That's why they hardly criticize each other publicly. They are all indebted to each other.

Since I woke up from the teenage coma a couple of years ago, I have never heard or read any of them engaging each other in a decent disagreement over any national issue in the media.

The Transitional Constitution of the Republic of South Sudan which was brought to existence by some of the clique's learned members prohibits them from dealing in any profit-making projects, a trashy provision they seemingly smilingly dust off their shoulders. It decrees that:

"The President, Vice President, Presidential Advisors, Ministers, and Deputy Ministers of the National Government, Governors, state Advisors, state Ministers, and other constitutional office holders shall, during their tenure of office, neither practice any private profession, transact commercial business, nor receive remuneration or accept employment of any kind from any source other than the National Government or a state government as the case may be."

Who amongst the senior civil servants is not running a commercial business, in or outside the country or both? The person who made that a law wasn't foolish. He knew what it is like to mix civil service with personal business programs. When you're a businessman, honesty flies out through the roof. You become susceptible to cheating. Pillage becomes your hobby.

In February 2012, a dubious written order exempting Vivacell, the largest mobile telephony company, from paying taxes for a period of about ten years got leaked:

"....the licensor hereby ensures to the licensee that the license is granted tax exemptions for a period of ten years at least, such tax exemption include custom duties, income taxes, sale taxes, etc. or any other taxes which may be imposed in the near future such as Value Added Taxes and the Licensor undertakes to indemnify the license in full in that respect. As such, the excise tax is not applicable on Vivacell."

Why would the government free such an income generating company from taxes? Who owns Vivacell anyway? Is he an ordinary businessman or a senior government official, a South Sudanese or a foreign national?

On Wednesday, the Finance minister, after being fried, roasted and tossed around by the Parliamentary Public Accounts Committee over misappropriated millions of dollars he disbursed to some company, rightfully snitched on His Excellency:

"Yes, the money was disbursed, no contract agreement, the disbursement was based on the strength of the letter of H.E the President."

Very freaking unbelievable!! Did the President actually sign that paper himself or someone forged his signature? Or did someone lure the old man into such a self-degrading act?

In November 2008, a Lebanese paper carried a story about high-profiled SPLA generals on a visit to Beirut. The Generals, who are currently holding ministerial positions in the government, went to check out the progress of their 25 companies that they had created some years back. Beirut Business Weekly quoted a Lebanese official as saying:

"This significant visit will definitely help bring the two trading partners businessmen closer and also help strengthen the trading ties between Lebanese Businessmen and SPLA generals... Lebanese foreign trade with SPLA reached US 11.085 million in 2006 to 2007. There are 25 SPLA companies operating in Beirut and are registered with the Chamber."

Are those companies public or private? Ain't Lebanon the pit latrine where the SPLA soldiers' salaries were intentionally dumped into, forcing the freedom fighters to become herbivorous, mango and grass eaters?

If SPLM wasn't a group of freemasons, who among them would need a degree in rocket sciences to figure out deliberate violations of the law by his or her colleagues? If the SPLM wasn't an acephalous organization of hardcore official criminals whose members find pleasure in illicit activities they do without fear of rebuke and severe punishment, who among them would hesitate to condemn the crimes committed by his colleagues; crimes that crippled and continue to cripple the young nation and its citizens?

Unless an internal ideological (as opposed to tribal) war erupts within my beloved party, the SPLM, democracy will remain a pipe dream. I don't have an idea what would cause such a war but I am very hopeful that it will happen. If it does break out, each influential official with presidential aspirations will civilly walk away and form his or her own political party with a manifesto, aimed at attracting all South Sudanese, despite tribal marks, height, weight, belly-size and et cetera.

The President Seeks a Protégé

April 13, 2014

I, PRESIDENT SALVA KIIR MAYARDIT, MUST SAY ENOUGH IS ENOUGH. It's about time I did the right thing – get out of the way. I will explain that shortly. First of all, know that I am speaking to you in this piece as a citizen. Forget about the Lt. General in me. Don't even think about my position as the President. This is the real me, the son of a Fishing Spear - Salva Kiir Mayardit, Kuethpiny.

Yes, I have to edge out of the way, along with my comrades. The spirit of a true soldier, a freedom fighter, has finally dawned on me. When I joined the liberation struggle over three decades ago, I did it for the right cause. I wanted South Sudanese to be whatever they wanted to be – Christians, Moslems, Buddhists or even devil-worshippers.

I was up against the systematic abuses meted out against them by the successive suppressive Khartoum governments. I fought day and night. Unlike some of my peers, I never looked back. Bush was my home, for years. Alongside my fellow freedom fighters, I fought fearlessly, tirelessly.

Yet I expected nothing in return. My actions were all sacrificial. So were my comrades'. We never dreamt about salaries. We never expected things like V-8s. We never thought about the lavish lifestyle we are living right now.

We never wanted to be rulers after the war. No, that was not part of our plan. I didn't want to be a payam administrator, let alone being a president.

As you may know, not everything goes according to plan. I am the President of South Sudan by default. I never wished to lead. The seat issue caught me off-guard. John Garang's death created a power vacuum. With the Generals choking with power-greed, a controversy arose over the throne. Every high-ranking SPLA official, except me, wanted to be the one.

But as fate would have it, the volatile region wanted a cool, calm and humble leader. Southern Sudan wanted a peace-maker leader. This made some influential but wise Generals force me onto the throne.

The decisions I have made, the actions I have taken for the last eight and half years proved those generals right. President Bashir has tried and is still trying harder to make me wage war against his country, in vain, simply because of my cool nature. I simply brush off his war-provoking actions and statements.

Some of my peers have tried to sow seeds of discord amongst

South Sudanese citizens but because of the cool me, I break the backbone of the divisiveness by doing what I am not going to tell you in this write up.

I have been called names by everyone including children. Boys and girls post insulting and defamatory articles about me on the internet. But I take it easy. All I say is: Lord, forgive them for they do not know what they are doing.

Even my comrades, those whom I suffered with in the bush unwittingly took up arms against my administration and ironically butchered the same people they liberated. I liken them to a father who fathers five children and wakes up one morning to slaughter them.

This unnecessary armed opposition is clearly meant to taint the image of my young government.

Others, the ones I entrusted with my powers, those I thought would assist me raise South Sudan to the world standards have shamelessly ungratefully institutionalized bad governance. They steal public funds. They like money but shun work. Everyone wants to fly to Nairobi, Dubai or Europe for flu treatment.

As a result, I have decided to rid the government of the freedom fighters turned looters. Yes I am decided. I want to replace them with vibrant youth. Youth because my generation does not fit in this era, particularly governing. These are modern times. All world governments have gone digital, technological. This, itself, disqualifies us.

Just drop by the Ministries. Visit the Immigration department in Juba-dit. The old men have been chased away by the new technology. They can't handle any work involving computers. Young people have taken over. All the old ones do is sign documents.

This rings a bell. Corruption, ineptness and technological incapacitation are enough reasons to retire my age mates.

This is how we will go about it: South Sudanese youth all over the world must converge to bring their representative. The young person must be a highly educated one. He must be strictly between the ages of 30 and 35, someone who is eloquent, exposed, humble, honest, detribalized and preferably a non-Dinka. He or she must be conversant with the political, social and economic affairs of South Sudan, both the past and the present. More importantly, he mustn't be an SPLM supporter. A teetotaler too.

This is because a 30-year old is too young to have relationships with the corrupt old guys. The same with the SPLM; if he or she comes from the SPLM, old bad guys will always want to stick their noses into his affairs in many ways.

I believe in meritocracy but I strongly believe that a non-Dinka would play a vital role in national healing process. Don't get me wrong. A non-Dinka president would heal the scariest wounds of the past which seem to dog the present.

One of them is the born-to-rule adage. I often hear about it. Since the agents of divide have successfully drummed it into the heads of many South Sudanese, mostly the semi-literates, I believe helping an Acholi, a Bari, a Lokorong, a Balanda or an Anyuak become the next president would nullify such a bad politics.

Another wound is: people say that the Dinka people say they will run the country until the end of time just because they sacrificed a lot during the civil war – that they died in big numbers-millions, and now is the payback time. I think that is not true. That hearsay is meant to indoctrinate the Dinka against the other tribes. Bringing up a Madi or a Jur Beli would put such people to shame.

Why a teetotaler? – A drunken head of state is susceptible to numerous grave mistakes. Bad people, mostly his or her relatives or friends, tend to lure him into signing dubious documents under the influence of alcohol. I am not speaking from experience but that is a fact, a proven one.

With the 2015 general elections in mind, I will work with the young candidate. I will help the young man or woman found a political party to contest against the frail SPLM. And I am counting on the youth to campaign for the new party and vote overwhelmingly for him or her.

If he or she wins and of course it must, youth will also help appoint qualified South Sudanese as members of his cabinet.

If the 'baby' president wishes, some of us, very few, will remain in the government but as advisors only.

I know Vice President Riek is itching to be the next president but don't worry about him. I will convince him. I will talk him out of the whole idea. I acknowledge how hard it is, almost impossible for him to stand down still, nothing is impossible. He himself should know without being told that to be the second most powerful man in the land is itself enough to go for the last top place.

In fact, he has handled a number of national issues a lot more than I have done. If he still itches to lead, then pride must be the only force driving his quest – pride and prestige, things South Sudan does not need right now.

So, my dearest youth, find me a young person that fits the above descriptions. You have a couple of months to produce him/her.

Verbal Draconian Traffic Laws

June 8, 2019

Dear Michael Chiengjiek, the minister of interior, you do not pay (well) your boys and girls in white uniform. As a result, they line up by every road and street in Juba day in day out (as early as 4am) to pull over motorists with the sole intent to beg for or demand money over issues unrelated to traffic offenses such as driving while wearing dreadlocks or vest.

But then, the motorists, with time, started refusing to entertain the nonsensical mendacity and extortion by driving on. Now, you are saying your boys and girls must open fire on drivers. Okay.

Honorable Minister, you based your decision on tinted window "menace" - that criminals hide behind those shaded windows as they execute their plots. Really?

This is preposterous. First of all, there are two types of tints, namely: the shade and factory tints. The dark shade is fitted on windows here in Juba. It's removable. I understand such heavily tinted vehicles are driven by security agents, particularly the omnipotent national security boys.

Factory tint is a thin shade that comes with cars from Japan. It's irremovable. These vehicles are imported mostly by young men and women in the private sector.

They are approved by your ministry to enter the country the way they are. And these particular vehicles, mostly Subaru, have been an issue with your ministry officials who believe that they are used to carry "people's wives and daughters" – a very archaic (7th century) thinking.

By the way, when did it become traffic police's business to ensure that no one carries somebody else' wife or daughter?

You and other senior officials at your ministry also believe that only the non-V8 vehicles are used by "criminals" to execute their criminal activities. And with your line of thinking, everyone is a gangster and must be gunned down. Okay.

Well, it appears that you do not know what you are talking about. The citizens you wish death upon are some of the main pillars of this economy. Actually, they are the reason the sick economy has not left the ICU for mortuary. Think. They are a very productive lot. They work 8 to 5 for companies, local and international NGOs and UN agencies. They pay taxes, taxes that are pocketed by your peers.

This and previous orders are illegal and call for defiance because you are basing them on your individual emotions. Mr. Draco, this is 21st century. Rules and orders must be based on legislations, not emotions. The Traffic Act, 2003 does not mention tinted windows. If you want to operate within the law, have your emotions discussed at the TNLA.

Therefore, the order to shoot lawfully defiant motorists is criminal itself and you should be held accountable for such a reckless irresponsible utterance you call order.

Misplaced Loyalty

August 26, 2016

WE (THE YOUTH) HAVE BLINDLY OFFERED SOUTH SUDAN'S GOOD-FOR-nothing leaders so much respect, defense, and value they don't deserve, for so long. All this happens in different forms and colors.

Out of tribalism and misplaced loyalty, we are quick to get guns and pens to fight for Dr Riek and Kiir, the men who have both failed the country. They fail us when they are working together. They also fail us when they're in conflict.

President Kiir, a man who is torn apart between hagiocracy-democracy and dictatorship, just cannot consolidate power. He has blatantly refused to take charge of the country's affairs.

He's like a housewife who just sits there and watches her young children break things in the house – china, TV, and glasses

– without disciplining them. "What am I gonna do with these children," she lazily says. Well, beat their asses, cow.

Dr Riek, on the other hand, is a curse. A well-educated man, Dr Riek ironically has nothing to show for his doctorate. He's a lamebrained politician who doesn't know how to avoid violent political game.

Needless to mention his past records, he's too dull to succeed Kiir. He doesn't know how to play political chess game. Kiir has checkmated him several times now. In the latest, instead of staying at the palace until the palatial gunfight incident was resolved, he stupidly opted to return to his place. Checkmate!

***

Anyway, Kiir-Riek political rivalry has kinda 'forcefully' divided youth into two unorganized groups: government and Dr Riek supporters.

Note that there's no neutral ground to stand here. Anyone who claims to be neutral is cheating him/herself. Not even activists and "nationalists".

Take for example Jon Pen. Mr Pen considers himself an activist. He claims that he's a nationalist too. Ok. But what baffles inquisitive souls is his "activism" records. The e-activist attacks President Kiir and government officials only. He's never ever 'touched' Dr Riek and the G-10. He actually praises and defends them in his writings.

Mr Pen and his IO followers also poke out eyes of those whose views are not in favor of Pagan, Dr Riek, and Dr Majak and all of the other political no-hopers.

Of late, they've been vituperating and terrorizing Citizen Mading Ngor Akec Kuai for airing his views on topical matters.

Well, since they are politically intolerant, how and why do they expect Kiir to accommodate dissenting voices such as that of Pen?

Pen must be neutral, mentally. His actions are ever partial. What he writes about shows that he's IO and G-10 activist, a position no one should be ashamed of. It's okay to fight for a cause, but just know where you stand. Pen does not know what side he belongs.

Many would liken him to a brain-in-a-jar. In philosophy, there is a brain-in-a-vat/jar skeptical argument. This is a thought experiment deployed to explain "radical skepticism", the view that we don't know nearly as much as we think we do.

***

As such, this chapter of our country's history is a messy one and requiring us to think harder and make tough choices.

Look. The country is now in a very bad shape, politically, economically, and socially. The upheaval we are facing is attributable to power, hunger for political power. Dr Riek and the bunch of ex-government officials want to dethrone Kiir by force or through some blemished international policies.

But none of these attempts to oust Kiir will succeed because he owns all the state resources: money, weaponry, foreign allies, and soldiers. He cannot be removed violently. He cannot step down either because his powerful circles won't allow. Why? Because they're feeding, even thriving, on his very weaknesses as a leader.

More importantly, power wrangles bring about friction and the outcomes are always despicable. Though most people don't see it in the news, many soldiers are killed in the battles.

Civilians are fleeing to IDP and refugee camps whereby they suffer poor health, poor feeding, and other inhumane living conditions.

Properties and businesses have been destroyed. Economy has been hospitalized in an Intensive Care Unit. Young entrepreneurs who were busy making their lives have been reduced to nothing. Citizens are hungry. Only few people afford decent meals. Pauperism is on the rise. Foreign investment is no more.

The government diverts the budget to the war zone spending a huge sum on military supplies.

All these problems will recur for a very long period of time unless we do something as citizens and that is to stop listening to ex-officials. Yes Kiir is a devil, but a better one. Without anyone trying to steal his chair, we enjoy a relative peace.

Even though he wasn't engaged in development of the country, young people were thriving before the crisis. Businesses were booming. Many managed to elevate their living standards – they built houses, they bought expensive cars, they got married.

Now due to the political disturbance, young families are broken; houses and cars have been sold at throwaway prices to buy basic needs.

Just because the United Nations buys the disgruntled politicians' ideas doesn't mean they are right. Who knows the UN's intentions?

Stop listening to the likes of Riek, Majak, Pagan, Lam, because they are just like Kiir. None of them has the country at heart and they know it. They don't care about anyone. If any of them seized leadership today, they would just look after themselves.

The more we entertain these politicians, the more we will bleed. Remember Kiir will not rule forever. He'll leave the office someday. Let's not be driven by revenge, anger, and myopic thinking. Patience pays.

Educate, Do not Annihilate

Jan 28, 2019

MURLE IS AN ACEPHALOUS TRIBE. THE WORD ACEPHALOUS MEANS having no head. But anthropologists describe an acephalous society as a society which lacks political leaders or hierarchies.

A research on Murle conducted by David Turton in the late 1970s shows that Murle views every other tribe as a foe. They call them "moden", loosely meaning enemy. This means a non-Murle is automatically an enemy, and thus must be dealt with.

Some of these modens have organized and executed retaliatory attacks against Murle. Lou Nuer attacked Murle land in 2011 and so did Bor in 2017.

However, Murle tribesmen keep going back to maim, kill,

torch villages and drive away cattle. Note that it's not every Murle that carries out attack on Lou Nuer, Dinka, Jie, Anyuak and any other neighbor of theirs.

These are just the recent incidents. A thousand others took place before Salva Kiir, David Yau Yau, and Tearz came into existence.

In Bor, delinquent young people are frowned at. It's every adult's responsibility to stop any young man from committing crime, including larceny, scuffle, rape and disobedience. Chiefs are respected. They hear cases. They fine wrongdoers. That's the way of life in Bor.

On the other hand, Murle community is acephalous. Traditional leaders have no say in someone else's business. They don't have the power to talk sense into youth. A group of youth raids a cattle camp and drives the loot (cows) to Buma where no one punishes them.

Basically, their way of life remains unchanged since they arrived in the present day Buma. They fight. They raid. They avenge.

This means more people will continue to die, huts will continue to burn, women will continue to cry, and cattle will continue to be raided forever unless the modens do something about it.

The Murle have been probably unable to change all this time due to their location which is generally too hidden for civilization to reach.

So, as people who are a little bit ahead in terms of modernity, you should not fight back but sit down together as one people (Dinka Bor, Lou Nuer and Jie) and think of a way to put this problem to an end.

Personally, I would second John Garang's vision: "Take towns to the people." This could take a very long time, a century, to realize but it's worth it.

No Children
in South Sudan,
No Gov't Position

March 19, 2013

UNLESS EVERY CONSTITUTIONAL POST HOLDER REPATRIATES HIS OR
family to South Sudan, efforts to build the country will always go
to waste.

   To serve one's country equals serving one's immediate family. In
essence, a leader is two fathers in one. He has two families that he
looks after, cater for. One family is comprised of wife and children.
The other comprises of you and me and his immediate family as

well. A good leader serves his nation the very way he serves his immediate family. Such a leader is called real patriot.

But as the saying goes: no one can serve two masters, it is really hard, almost impossible, for a leader, particularly a South Sudanese, to serve his nation efficiently, especially when his wife and children are residing in a foreign land.

An immediate family, mainly children, play a major role in the ruling of a nation. Children influence decisions a leader makes on national issues. That's why it is rare to find a childless democratic leader today. If there are any, you will always learn that they have adopted children, honorary sons and daughters.

For South Sudan, it's different. The fact that children of senior government officials are still residents of foreign cities has serious implications on the way the country is being governed. It's simple:

When children of a cabinet minister go to a private school in Nairobi or Kampala, he or she will always pay little or no attention at all to challenges facing primary school children in Chukudum or Nasir.

When his son goes to one of the top colleges in New York or London, whatever problem that faces Juba or Wau university students, whatever plight he hears 'gets into his head through one ear and flies out through the other'.

When young children and the elderly die at Juba Teaching Hospital due to lack of medical supplies, when mothers die during delivery at Malakal civil Hospital because there is no one to attend to them for nurses have downed their tools over salary arrears, you cease to listen because none of your family members is affected in any way.

When majority of Juba residents, after eight years, 'smell' electricity. When the citizens are losing hearing to the deafening sound of Chinese generators, you find it too much work to devise solutions simply because neither you nor your child knows what it feels like to dwell in a town without power.

When good citizens die in road carnages due to bad roads, when a rescue team takes three days to get to a 10 kilometer far off village to fight off raiders because of non-existence of road networks, you knock back three tots of your favorite European whiskey and say "who cares?" because none of your children uses those roads.

When almost every home in Juba does not have access to running water, when women still walk distance to fetch water, none of those conditions inspires you to find possible solutions to the prolonged suffering because you're your family is enjoying sweat of other men who toiled, men who built landmarks to make sure their offspring have something to brag about.

Do you see how your children are impacting on the national issues, directly?

Yes every parent wants best things for his or her children. Every father wants his children to acquire better education. But now that all these are impacting on the nation negatively, won't you move your family back to the country?

It sounds wild but the moment you use economic lens to look at it, you will get to realize how destructive this is to the country. If school fees of a government official is Ksh. 100,000 per term, do you know what it means to the young economy of South Sudan?

If a civil servant sends tens of thousands of dollars to Australia or America monthly or so, do you know how bad it is to the economy?

If a constitutional post holder, someone charged with the responsibility of building the nation, can buy a 20-million-shilling mansion in Nairobi, how many other comrades of his have such houses? And how bad is it to the country?

Elevation of the baby country is easy. It doesn't require rocket science to better it. All it needs is heart, patriotism.

Since school is one of the shields these men always defend themselves with, improvement and transformation of the education sector must be prioritized. Below are possible solutions.

But first, let's first look at how bad the education sector is. A UNESCO recent report highlights factors behind low enrollment and early drop out vary across states. The two factors most widely reported by parents for their children being out of school are cost and distance.

While the government has a nominal policy of free basic education, many schools appear to levy charges. Moreover, parents face indirect costs associated with the purchase of uniforms and books. Distance is especially problematic in states – such as Western Bar Ghazal, Western equatorial and Jonglei – with low population densities.

In the case of South Sudan, infrastructure deficits and shortages of learning materials reinforce deficits in the quality of education, as illustrated by the following data:

Pupil-teacher ratios are very high, especially for trained teachers. The national average ratio for pupils-trained teachers is 1:117, rising to 1:141 in Unity and Upper Nile states and 1:201 in Jonglei.

Classroom shortages are pervasive. One third of the children 'in school' are being taught in the open air and another quarter in semi-permanent or basic classrooms. The average pupil classroom ratio is 134:1

Provision of latrines and safe drinking water is limited, with just half of schools having access to both facilities. Most school children ease themselves in the nearby bushes.

Textbooks are in short supply, with an average pupil

textbook ratio of 1:4 rising to the worst case scenario of 1:9 in Unity state.

The above problems mirror the government's perception of the education sector. It devalues the badly needed education.

A problem well defined is a problem half-solved. Well, need I describe how the government should solve the remaining half? No.

PART II

SOCIAL ISSUES

Bad Economy-induced Dialectical Assimilation

June 5, 2015

HEHE. WHAT'S HAPPENING IN JUBA RIGHT NOW REMINDS ME OF one evolution theory that I learnt about in high school. Or was it primary school? Damn. My memory is dull. Or have I aged already? I didn't like biology, anyway. I'm talking about survival of the fittest.

Life's getting harder in Juba. To survive, some non-Barkazeel are now learning how to speak thong Barkazeel (Dinka Rek dialect). Let me explain.

This crisis has affected every citizen in one way or another. Domino effect unarguably applies here.

In South Sudan, specifically in Juba, economy is dying. Others would say it's already dead. Businesses are collapsing. Others have already collapsed, dead and RIPed.

Market prices, like Jesus in Jewish mythology, have ascended. You would need a telescope to see some of them. Again, some basic market commodities are scarce. Thanks to US dollars. Fuel is hoarded by oil dealers. Some people have parked their cars. They walk to work. Others have sold their vehicles at throw-away prices to meet other living costs.

Irrespective of all that, salaries remain the same. People are desperate, broke. Those who were able to afford a beer bottle before just can't afford now.

Rich businessmen and senior government officials who used to pelt friends and relatives with bundles of money for fun have changed their phone numbers.

Others have moved to hotels. Why? To avoid platoons of relatives who keep knocking on their doors to tell them stories about their own problems.

Virtues and values are gone. And honesty is the first casualty. And this is widespread in the business community. Cheating, especially amongst businesspeople, is on the rise. Friends are setting up friends in fake deals. Some have been jailed for failing to repay huge amounts in loan. That's the general state of affairs.

I don't know why some of non-Barkazeel are undergoing dialectical assimilation right now but think about Aristotle's' deductive reasoning. I believe Barkazeel monopolize public money, power and influence.

In order to get a business deal, a contract, one needs to get close to or use some influential friend from there to push for it. To get into his or her head, you need to bribe him psychologically – appease him. So, speak some Apuk or Aguok or Awan Chan or Kuach, speak your way to big fat government deals. Lol. 'Aye wentui' 'Mith apol?' 'Ci bak?' 'Kontrak dan awar to kedi?' lol!

∎

Recently, a scuffle between a pedestrian and a motorist caused a huge scene in Juba, along Tombura Road. A man charged at a Nissan X-trail driver, reached for his throat and dragged him out of the car, head-butted him right in the nose, turning it into a blood tap. He beat him into a one-minute coma.

People rushed in and pulled him away. When asked why, he shamelessly said: "He refused to let me cross." And he walked off. Really?

The driver cut off the man from crossing the road, according to eyewitnesses. As fate would have it, a traffic jam built up just about 200 meters away from the point the would-be attacker tried to cross.

So, the driver slowed down and eventually come to a complete halt. He was just there, seated in the car, in the jam, listening to music. And that's when the man descended.

Why would I fight a motorist for ignoring my signal to allow me to cross the road? What amount of anger?

I'm not saying that the attacker had some sort of bad-economy-induced-trauma but you never know. With these crises, economic crisis, to be particular – everyone is getting his or her share, in one way or another. It comes in different shapes, sizes, and colors.

If this general situation persists, though, some of us surely will relocate to the UN camps in order to get free meals. Lol.

∎

However, as young people who do not wish to see or imagine this country come down to its knees in the nearest future, we tend to refuse to acknowledge the negative impact of the SPLM war of seats has had on the people of South Sudan as a whole.

Irrespective of the dying economy that comes as a result of ever wanting leadership, we still tend to make others, particularly the anti-government brothers, believe that the war hasn't affected us in anyway – that everything is alright.

We still dress up smartly, hop into our rickety Japanese-made SUVs and sedans, and drive to work places just like before. We still crack jokes with our colleagues in office as we work.

As youth - Nuer, Bari, Shilluk, Dinka, name it - we still gather at nearby food joints whereby we dip our fingers in the same dishes as colleagues. In the evening, we offer lift to friends or colleagues.

We still worship our nightlife. On weekends, we put on tight outfits and dash to our favorite joints – The Mask, Signature, Nile Secret, Panafric, etc – where we try to dance, drink and smoke away the realities of South Sudan.

The Dangers of shopping for girls in Africa

August 20, 2012

DEAR LOST BOYS, IT IS NOT WORTH IT. STOP IT! A GIRL IS A GIRL. IF you cannot find a marriageable South Sudanese sweet girl wherever you are - be it United States, Canada, Australia, New Zealand or United Kingdom, please try any other African girl or even a Latino, African American, Spanish or Chinese or Aboriginal. If none suits you at all, try celibacy. Just remain single for the rest of your life. Won't you?

A Jamaican journalist and politician, Marcus Garvey once said that, "A people without the knowledge of their past history, origin and culture is like a tree without roots." That is true. But what good is a culture that slaps you in the face for living it?

What good is a tradition that nullifies your efforts, a tradition that bears no fruits? So, why would you hold on to a culture that "pelts you with stones" every time you try to do things in accordance with its norms? Tell me why?

Your fellow Lost Boys who left Africa in their mid-20s quickly felt the urge to start a family. They worked themselves lame; working during the night and learning during the day as they manufactured "dowries". When they had saved enough money, they asked their cousins back in Africa to find beautiful girls to marry. And yes, the cousins did find girls.

The dudes flew in to finalize matrimonial arrangements. In Kenya, they paid millions of shillings to the brides' parents. Unfortunately, greed and pride set in. The poor guys were made to compete against one another in a bid to fleece them of money. He who presented more millions was awarded the girl while the loser embarked on another shopping spree until he found another girl whose parents had "small hearts".

The competition over bride wealth also bred conflict amongst clans. The defeated dude would elope with or abduct the controversial girl. This would flare up deadly clashes which at times left many people dead and others seriously injured, mainly at Kakuma camp.

Well and good. They quickly began resettlement process for their spouses. Many young wives relocated to US where they were reunited with their husbands, while others moved to Australia, along with their siblings. Another group of Lost Boys opted to rent houses in Nairobi and Kampala where their sweethearts lived, and some still do, with their mothers and brothers and sisters.

The same Lost Boys sent their brothers in-law to "Kenyan schools." Some of the sponsored in-laws just graduated from good Kenyan universities and others are yet to graduate. And the fathers-in-law moved to South Sudan where they received part of bride prices in form of cattle. Some of these in-laws spent the millions on more cattle and resumed pastoralist lifestyle in cattle camps.

The urbane and enterprising in-laws ventured into business; they opened retail shops, restaurants and bars. Some even bought big trucks for business. And of course they prospered. Others squandered the bride wealth on alcohol and many other unimportant non-profit-making programs.

Do you see how your fellow Lost Boys helped elevate lives? Do you see the socio-economic role they played, play?

On the other hand, things do turn rough and unfavorable to most Lost Boys. A lot of uncertainties set in, unexpectedly. In this account, I am going to categorize Lost Boys' misfortunes and problems under wives, four types of wives. Let's nickname them "nyanbots." Nyanbot is a Dinka word that can loosely mean a girl worthy of 100 heads of cattle.

The-do-not-get-along-with nyanbots: Some nyanbots that joined their husbands in the Unites States do not keep the marriage vows. After a brief union, disagreements crop up. This is because the dudes never courted them at least to know them in and out before making them their wives. They got them through cousins or parents. So, when the daily drama in the house crescendoes and becomes unbearable, a nyanbot walks away, taking away the children.

United States government policies are superb; the authorities normally take care of poor immigrant families. Therefore, she is thrown on Welfare with her kids until another man falls for her. Count that as a loss to Lost Boys.

The 'temporarily infertile' nyanbots; the other group of Lost Boys are never lucky enough to beget children with their nyanbots. The dudes use a lot of money on air tickets, to and fro, occasionally visiting Africa. In all the visits, a Lost Boy moves from hospital to hospital, city to city with his nyanbot, seeking treatment for the condition; impotence or barrenness, I don't know.

But unconfirmed report from people says Lost Boys swallow 'anti-child' tablets before boarding a plane to Africa. They have not told me why. And others say nyanbots swallow pills instead of using condoms, in their quest to fight unwanted pregnancies. Swallowing of those drugs comes about when a nyanbot decides to "kiss her former boyfriend (you can add letter S if you like) goodbye," knowing that the Lost Boy will come soon to take her away.

The pills have a long lasting effect on the reproductive system, depending on the type one swallows. Some can last as long as five years or more. I find truth here because after some marriages got dissolved some years ago, certain nyanbots did later bear children with different men, and some Lost Boys fathered children with new girls.

Needless to say the important role played by a child in a marriage relationship, the two find no peace in the union; hence, the marriage goes up in a smoke. That is another loss to Lost Boys, a mountain of loss.

The promiscuous nyanbots: 'We' have witnessed many Lost Boys call it quits due to unfaithfulness in their nyanbots. Partly blame that on distance love. When they leave their young wives behind, irrespective of material love they shower them with, some nyanbots find it hard or impossible to live up to marriage vows.

When some an anonymous wise man excogitated the saying, "Out of sight, out of mind," tens of millennia ago, I wonder if he had Lost Boys and their nyanbots on his mind. While her loving husband serves voluntary life imprisonment abroad, in form of hard work, just to make her live a better life in Nairobi, Eldoret, Nakuru, Jinja or Kampala, a nyanbot chooses to cheat on him. She quickly rekindles love affair with her ex- boyfriends (you can remove letter S if you like). They do wild things together. They drink. They rev.

And they even smoke marijuana together. Some of the nyanbots revisit girlhood and make new boyfriends, mostly young guys, niggas, who normally have stronger sexual stamina. They usually spend Lost Boys' hard earned cash on them; mostly on expensive skinny jeans, shoes and alcohol. Again, Lost Boys lose here.

The real nyanbots: Nevertheless, some Lost Boys do get married to nice nyanbots - nyanbots that are impeccable, adaptable. Once they get married, they intentionally wisely lose contact with their former boyfriends and religiously dedicate their bodies, minds and time to their husbands. They are now living happy lives, whether they are living apart or not. Remember, this group of nyanbots has the tiniest number of girls Lost Boys shopped for in Africa.

In my mind, I see the Lost Boys as a group of good people caught between the end of one civilization and the beginning of another. They are being sandwiched between the two conflicting giant cultures. It's a total mess. The ending civilization forces them to marry their parents' choices. Unfortunately, those girls belong in the new civilization where freedom of choice tops the list of all freedoms.

The fact that most marriages that involve Lost Boys do not last long is simple. The girls they marry are found through connections.

There is never any courtship involved. There is never any love, no romance. Their chemistry is ever wrong from the start. A Lost Boy's mother calls him up and goes like: "my son, I saw the daughter of Chol-dit yesterday at the church.

She is a sweet little girl. She is brown-skinned and has a beautiful gap between her teeth. She has big thighs too. She also has big breasts, the size of calabash. I think she can make a good wife." Without hesitation, the dude sheepishly okays the proposition. Months or so later, he flies in with a lot of money to take his bride. Where is the love?

Girls' parents are the worst catalyst in the whole thing. With money on their mind, most of them are always ready to say yes to any man who proposes marriage to their daughters, regardless of what the girl thinks about it. How do you expect such a marriage to last forever? Yes, many families break up in every corner of the planet but it is a little over exaggerated in the Lost Boys' world.

In addition to huge amounts of monies lost and time wasted, jilted, heart-broken, drained, traumatized and dejected, a Lost Boy sinks beneath the sea of regret.

So, tell me my brother, where do you want to belong above? Remember, chances of you finding a real nyanbot are slim.

Tearz Travel Advisory

November 22, 2012

As Christmas season tiptoes in, I would love to advise those who are planning to spend the happy holiday with relatives and old friends in South Sudan. Call it Tearz Travel Advice or TTA in short. But remember, this is not mandatory, it is recommendatory. You have what it takes to take it or leave it.

You must have read or heard from friends that the baby country is growing except that it is developing at a speed of a snail. No, I am sorry I lied. Snail is faster than the speed at which development is moving in this country. This is because your, no, I mean our uncles and aunts are squandering the monies that come from oil revenues and sympathizers like the European Union and Unites States, amongst others.

When you touch down at Juba International Airport, your sensors will quickly notify you that you're in a strange place. High humidity is the first thing that will say to you, "Hello, welcome to Juba my long lost friend." Your skin will not like the new condition, hence you will leak.

English people call it sweating. The airport is a bit disorganized. Non-travelers walk in and out of the immigration sector. You can, for whatever reason, choose to bypass the immigration desk, depending on your body features.

By the time you walk out of the terminal, your outfit will have soaked from sweat. From the airport, you will either head home or straight to a hotel, depending on the size of your purse or the protrusion of your belly.

Hotel

Hotels are very expensive. Accommodation costs over 100$ per night. Despite the fact that Juba hotels are not up to the western standards, they are somewhat decent. Each room has that device which dehumidifies the air. There is a water shower, clean tiled-floor, comfy king-size bed and fan, TV set and a fridge. However, I would not urge you to eat from those hotels.

Most of the foods they offer are those that have overstayed

in fridges. Nutritional value is gone. No taste at all. By the way, after spending a very long period of time away from South Sudan, what would stop you from mingling with Jubans in local restaurants where you can find kisra, korob-lubia, asida made from cassava, awal-wala served with fermented milk, akop, dried fish and original fresh Tilapia or Nile Perch from the Nile River?

Modern Home

For my friend who will take a taxi home, welcome to Juba, buddy. This is where you will experience most of the things you heard about South Sudan. And if you're a keen observer, your stay at your uncle's place could give you an idea about the root cause of corruption.

If your uncle is a senior civil servant, you are safe. However, the only problem you will face is overcrowding. No privacy. Most rich government officials' homes which I call mini-refugee camps are ever overcrowded, making life a bit uneasy. Nieces, nephews, uncles, in-laws, friends, bodyguards and many others are the occupants. Some come from as far as Nairobi, Kampala, and villages to seek financial aid from one man - the uncle. "This boy needs school fees; that one needs to travel outside the country for a surgery. This woman wants to go back to her children in the village. That one over there seated on a mat arrived last night. They are all waiting for one man's salary, my salary," a minister once said.

And on payday, the big man distributes his salary to them, and both painfully and annoyingly enough, another hungrier contingent of relatives comes and camps. When it goes, another group arrives. The most annoying thing is that they carry their own mattresses, bed sheets and mosquito nets. That gives an uncle no room for lame excuses like "oh my house is congested, oh blah blah blah."

Life in a Tukul

For my buddy who may wish to have fun with friends in normal homes, ready yourself for some real fun. No electricity. No running water. No toilets. At night, mosquitoes rule. They make nights long and unbearable. They tax people; taxation is in form of blood.

If you're lucky enough, you may find a pit latrine in your host's compound. But please, always carry pieces of toilet paper in your pocket. It helps. In case you choose to ignore me, you stand a risk of scratching your buttocks with a twig. You were warned.

If your host lives in a place like Lubas-mafi or Rujal-mafi and doesn't have a latrine, expect the unexpected. This means you will be forced to relieve yourself at a neighbor's. Using a neighbor's latrine is not a problem because South Sudanese are still generous.

The issue is traffic. In Juba, many home owners consider latrine a luxury. A family of about ten members defecates in the nearby bushes or open grounds. That means when one man builds one for his family, all the neighboring homes will use it. So, to use such a latrine, you must queue up, particularly during morning hours. When you finally make it in, you could find something unusual.

You are likely to find fecal landmines on the slap. This means some girls used the latrine earlier. There is a belief in Juba that girls do not squat on the pit latrine lest they become barren. So, they plant a lot of fecal landmines on the floor. And some men do not clean toilet after use. They leave that thing swimming simply because of the I-am-not-the-cleaner mentality, I hear.

Your Foreign Currency/Exchange

In here, the cart goes before the horse. The Central Bank is impotent. Exchange rate is being controlled by cattle keepers. Isn't that weird? They decide when the pound rises or drops. Right now, the official dollar rate is 2.9 pounds per dollar. While in the black market; with one dollar, you get 4.2 pounds. Unconfirmed reports say the dollar business run by the cattle keepers is a big thing.

The herders are mere agents. Their bosses are in the government. And that's why the Juba City Council finds it hard to rid the city of them. Its efforts to arrest these official law breakers are thwarted by powerful anonymous caller who instructs the police to stop "harassing innocent civilians."

Some of these cattle keepers turned money exchangers are conmen. I call them dollar-rustlers. They possess counterfeit money, both pounds and dollars. Always take precautions. If possible, choose one of them and let him hop in a car you're riding in. With the help of your cousin or a friend, exchange your dollars. They operate in tree shades, at markets. In case you show up at their place, they will pretend to be cross checking the genuineness of your notes.

One dude holds it up to the light and feels it with his fingertips. He passes it on to another dude who does the same thing. By the time it comes back to you, it will have passed through hands of about ten dudes. Guess what happens? The one that comes back to you is a fake dollar bill. This is when they begin to reduce the rate and if you don't agree to it, they ask you to leave.

Generally, Juba is fun. It's the place to be during December holidays. Lots and lots of fun; all day all night - The social places, the party-goers, everything. However, things are a bit more different here. That means there are some things, habits that you need to leave behind:

Dress Code

And this goes to girls. I know you are used to doing things the western way. That's fine. It's your life, your choice. You're notorious for not wearing enough clothes – extremely provocative outfits: quarter-skirts (not mini- anymore) and string-like underpants. Some of you don't even wear underwear anymore.

Others put on tight and transparent bra-less tops that show nipples. That's cool. Some of us like that. But the problem is, when you dress up like that for a night party here, others, in fact, many, will think that you're a call girl. Not to mention how South Sudanese men behave when drunk, they would want to grab you by any part of you, teats first.

What do you think would happen to that social place should your male friends or brothers react? – A flying-bottle teeth-removal jaw-breaking zone, right? That's one.

Two, there has been reports about Juba Police harassing urbane females over dress code, especially those who wear tight jeans. Though it's not a legal thing to do, a small unit of police officers could anytime decide to 'teach' young people how to dress properly.

They normally stop them, confiscate the jeans and drive off. Guess who is standing by the roadside naked, on Christmas Day? – You! I have nothing much to say to you here but I would urge you to always carry extra clothes – skirts, long ones – in your handbag.

Accent

The way you speak English here matters a lot. Members of diaspora have lost lives to accent in the recent past. You know very well that the 21-year civil war has disadvantaged a big number of us. This has made it so hard for some people to see you as a brother or sister.

They feel intimidated, overlooked. So, when you speak that Lil Wayne or Nicki Minaj's accent while talking to police officers: "Hey worrap, maan? I jas came from the Unai stet, man. I am from Coloraro, man. Coloraro. It's a gu place, man. Youknowwhuramsayin? Aaight," someone might mistake that for conceit - that you're bragging about your academic acquisitions and maybe better life.

If you are not careful enough, your ribs or chest could be the perfect destination of flying blows, kicks and gun butts. Guess the aftermath of this encounter with the police, and make sure your guesswork is not far away from serious internal injuries, deformation and death.

Since you were not born in the United States, Australia, Canada or Europe, why can't you just speak in a normal way? If I were you, I would even speak our broken English: "Hawar you, polith opither? Yeth ah yam prom Thouth Thudan. My name will be Jamith Kalany. I am beri hepi por being home again." Would that hurt or cost you a dime? Good luck.

Wounded Pride

September 21, 2018

"RETURN THE MONEY TO THE GIRLS NOW," AN EMBARRASSED, ANGRY and gun-wielding man barked at a bartender, raising eyebrows at a bar in Juba recently. At first, patrons thought it was a heist.

He was suited up, pot-bellied, clean-shaven, and middle-aged - probably in his late 40s - the kind that makes money, lots of money, through fake government "Konturaks".

That evening, he arrived at the joint, alone, carrying a bunch of car keys and three smart phones. He ordered for a bottle of Krest soda and slices of lemon and began to sip it.

Thirty minutes or so later, he was joined by a bevy of girls, three in particular. They wined. They dined. They knocked back shots of Tequila. Laughed. They visited the loo in turns.

Later on, the man asked for the bill, which the barman placed on the table, 4 or so minutes later. However, the bill just stayed there, according to the barman's testimony.

When the girls realized that it was getting late and their host was taking forever to foot the bill, they figured out the problem – the O.G didn't have enough money.

"The meals, whiskey, wine and tequila ballooned the bill," recalled Barman X, "bringing the total to 113,750 Pounds."

So, the city chicks dipped their beautifully polished fingers into their handbags and dag up bundles of 100-Pound bills and handed it to the tender, wounding the dude's pride. He ran after the young barman with a pistol.

"Return the money to the girls now," he barked at the boy who seemed unshaken by the gun being held against his head.

"Why? What's wrong with the girls clearing the bill? They took the drinks and ate the food; thus, they have the right to pay, especially since you're not carrying cash," boldly said the boy.

The reply seemed to have sent extra bullets into the man's pride. He quickly cocked the pistol and shot in the air - forcing everyone, including the chicks, to run helter-skelter…

Ladies Shouldn't 'Gentlemanize' Boys

April 23, 2020

JUST LAST MONTH, SHORTLY BEFORE CORONAVIRUS FORCED UHURU Kenyatta to impose measures to prevent further spread of the pandemic, I hit the road, with the sole mission of sanitizing my throat. It was on a Friday. I actually wanted to go to Blackyz, but changed my mind. I sat at Bobo, below Mojos, and began to imbibe my ice cold beer.

Suddenly, a young couple walks in, hand in hand. They are probably 18 or so. I can smell the intimacy. The girl's eyes exude admiration for the young man. In matching shirts, faded sky blue denims, they look adorable. They sit at the next table, next to each other.

"Get us two beers, both Tusker," she smilingly tells the barmaid. They have fun. The missy wraps her hand around her love, choking him with love in public. She whispers. He smiles. They do renditions of trendy love songs playing on television.

After the third round, she asks for the bill. The patootie opens her bag and fishes out two one-thousand shilling notes. We used to call Ksh1,000 "Ngiri" or "Ndovu" during the Sheng of our time. Now I don't know what it's called.

The baby girl folds the notes as she looks around to ensure that no one sees the 'gentlemanization' ceremony - a secret process between two people which lasts a microsecond. I swear you will not witness it if you're not street smart.

I pretentiously look away. But with the corner of my eye, I watch her sneak the boy the money, under the table. Hehehe. The boy-turned gentleman then foots the bill, with zeal. And off the lovebirds exit the tiny lounge.

Such a scene is a commonplace everywhere these days, especially among South Sudanese in Juba, Kampala and Nairobi.

Do not get me wrong. There is nothing wrong in splitting bills as lovers, nor is it unacceptable for a female partner to clear it all.

The problem is the resultant self-destruct among the gentle-manized. Thanks to what I would call love-induced individual dependency syndrome.

Naturally, a boy child – whether a black, white or yellow - is raised to be a man, to be a gentleman. Be it a rural or urban setting, he's taught to be able to first look after himself, his immediate family and the society.

According to traditional African society, a village boy learns how to herd goats or sheep or both. He ensures that he drives them to grazing land and water points. He protects them from wild animals. These are the same animals he feeds on – milk and meat.

Whenever a need arises, his parents sell one of the goats and use the money to buy him shoes or blankets. Today, a small boy from Dinka, Masai, Acholi, Pokot or Samburu herds his goats after school or weekend. These goats are sometimes sold and the proceeds spent on his tuition fees.

As time flies by, a goat boy grows into a man. His role changes. He begins to grow crops and look after cattle or camels. He takes them to places with green grass and enough water, and protects them from both wild animals and raiders. With the cows, he gets a wife. He grows crops. He raises his children. He's a productive member of the society.

On the other hand, a town boy is taken to school to become an engineer, journalist, doctor, banker, or designer. After completing his diploma or degree course. He finds himself a job or starts his own business with the help of his parents/guardians. He gets paid. He moves out. He saves. He does whatever he wants, including getting married. He raises his family. He's a productive member of the society.

Now, some young girls and women, whom I will refer to as gentlemanizers, are violating the natural process of manufacturing a man.

Most of these young women, according to observations and testimonies, are "self-made" businesswomen. Others are daughters of Juba-based politicians and business tycoons. They are "filthy rich".

With this riches, some gentlemanizers shift the gentlemanization from the first to fifth gear by offering the gentlemanized everything, including rent, food, clothes, shoes and even automobiles. They are turning young South Sudanese boys into beneficiaries of financial aid, which is in turn going to likely induce dependency syndrome. Worst of all, they are helping destroy South Sudan by producing an army of unproductive men.

By catering for these boys, the women indirectly prevent them from acquiring skills and knowledge. Even those who may have acquired some education no longer have it, for it has evaporated due to lack of application. All they know is to "shine" everyday – wearing the latest sneakers, sweatpants and expensive wrist watches – and going out every weekend.

What happens when a gentlemanizer based in Australia falls for another boy with bigger muscles and tighter six pack? What happens to this unskilled young man when his self-made entre-preneur's businesses collapse? Or her father runs out of millions of dollars after getting fired by President Salva Kiir?

All this is all about love. But love does not destroy; it elevates. If you really love somebody, you do not let them live for the moment. You build them up. Therefore, the ladies should ensure that these boys acquire some skills, if they really love them – make them stand on their own feet.

Hasn't God Punished (South) Sudanese Yet?

September 28, 2007

THE BIBLICAL MESSAGE WRITTEN IN THE BOOK OF PROPHET ISAIAH that says God shall unleash His tsunami of hate, anger and bring to ashes the people of Sudan, titled "God Shall Punish Sudan" is both gruesome and traumatic. It is a threat.

It could even be a religious conspiracy to eliminate the tall people. It kills me softly. It keeps me wondering; why is God to punish the strong and powerful nation, tall and smooth-skinned people living along the Nile River, feared all over the world? What sin or sins have the people of Sudan committed that they appear in the God's list of those who will taste His wrath? And when was that? What is the magnitude of the sin committed?

All right, when will God punish Sudan? Hasn't he punished the Sudanese yet? Isn't the God's law that might have been violated by the Sudanese not one of the Ten Commandments? If yes, isn't it forgivable? Isn't God forgiving?

It also keeps me guessing; perhaps the Sudanese of that time contributed to the enslavement of the God's chosen people, the Israelites, when they were in the land of Egypt. Or maybe warriors from one of the Sudan's kingdoms, let's say, Napata, walked distances, crossed the seas and beat the cream out of Jews, destroying them to nothing, a battle which I suspect the authors of the bible maliciously omitted. What really happened? Or is there any other Sudan other than the present day Sudan whose city is Juba? I am dazed and confused.

I know you would love to know who this inquisitive person is. Yes, I am tall and smooth-skinned, born somewhere along river Nile. Thus, I am the one Isaiah 18 talks about.

Every time I open that part of the bible, I feel sick. It nauseates me. I get discouraged. I feel like a patient, with some complicated diseases of the body systems, who got informed by a doctor of the number of days or months left to die.

In fact, it discourages me from reading the bible. What eats me up most is the Grammar; the title is in future form yet I feel already punished. From the time I was born to the very moment you are reading this sentence.

I was born during the war, in the jungle, where neither clinic nor hospital was heard of. Nothing scientific was in the vicinity accept war tanks and war artilleries. No vaccination no immunization no nothing against any childhood diseases and ailments. No birth certificate too. I don't know my birthday. Mama has no clear memory of where and when I was born. All she remembers is sound of gunshots and a tall tree she bore me under.

In addition, I was raised up in the forest. Just picture a baby born and brought up in the forest, where there are no drugs and medicines, no house to shelter from rain, no coverings at least to keep the cold away.....only breast milk. And how about the mother? What does she eat in order to keep the breast milk "factory" functional? Grass or mud? Who knows? Isn't it punishment? Yet the bible boldly insists, "God will punish Sudan."

Hasn't He punished the Sudanese yet? These tall and smooth-skinned people feared all over the world are scattered all over the world. Aren't they facing untold sufferings? Ain't they treated with contempt wherever they are? Hasn't God punished them yet?

How about the Sudanese you know of? Most of them are maimed. Many have lost limbs to the war. Some limp, some crawl. Aren't they half-creatures now? We have been and are still suffering.

Sudan has never been peaceful since time immemorial. She is constantly at war, internal war. It is like the manufacturers of war weapons produce them having Sudan in mind as the market. Very funny! All types of weapons, from a 9mm pistol to the most dangerous atomic bomb are there. And to prove it, go to Sudan and see for yourself what it is like. The ground is covered with exhaust war metals, all over. Everything has been ruined. All is debris.

It is obvious to everyone that God has punished, has been punishing the tall and smooth-skinned people, yes? And I know

I'm going to sound offbeat if I told you that the punishment is being exaggerated by Isaiah 18. Believe me; the fact that the title is in Future tense keeps the punishment fire blazing. Yes.

To get it right, let's do something about it. What do we do?

I've got an idea. That portion of the Holy Bible should be changed. I mean it! We've got to put it in past form like "God Has Punished Sudan". I may be evil or of little or no faith to say that but I am serious. Give me a break! Only God can judge me!

The best way of realizing this idea is by summoning the religious leaders; Buddhists, Muslims and Christians together for a prayer. The prayer should be said in unison and I suggest it goes like this: "Almighty father, you said no one must alter anything written in Your Holy Book lest he or she faces serious consequences. But Lord, we beg of you, allow us change only Isaiah 18 for it is a major threat to the Sudanese people, and in your Holy name we pray, Amen."

Thereafter, those religious heads should order publication of a new edition of the Holy Bible with everything in Isaiah 18 in "was" form. I assure you it could work. This would be a relief to the Sudanese people. There would be no more pain and sufferings. Peace, love and harmony shall then rein forever.

Revalue Girls: Save Lives

June 10, 2013
"A home without a daughter is like a river without a source."
Margaret Ogola, the River and the Source.

February 4, 2014

A GIRL CAN BE A DAUGHTER, A SISTER, A COUSIN, AN AUNT AND A prospective mother. That simple description alone shows how important a girl is.

In Dinka civilization, having sisters means a lot. It means a boy cannot participate in tedious house chores such as cooking, cleaning, fetching water and firewood and so on. They milk cows too. A girl also protects her kid-sisters against abuse and bullying.

When she hits a marriageable age, she attracts tens or hundreds of heads of cattle in marriage. The number of heads of cows she attracts depends on the status of her father and her looks - beauty. She reproduces, raises her children, and follows through the rest of the rite of passage.

All her brother does is playing all day with friends. He appears only when hunger "bites his stomach." Older boys look after goats and sheep at the nearby grazing fields while "rothii" tend herds of cattle in distant grazing land. Here they protect them against wild animals and raiders. Parents farm and work on other communal functions. Grandparents take care of little children. That is the daily life of a Dinka.

I believe such a division and distribution of workload is practiced by many other Nilotic communities, particularly the Nuer- the closest cousins of Dinka.

With the widespread introduction of modernization – mushrooming urban centers, schools, this way of life seems to be getting eroded rapidly. Every family member has something modern to tackle every morning. Both boys and girls go to school.

Both parents report to work stations – hospital, market, school, etc. Only 'Nyanluoi' remains behind to look after toddlers and maybe the aging. Some mothers go to school – adult education, computer training. Family members meet again later in the evening and disperse again the following morning.

Just like Dinka boys, Dinka girls go to school to become doctors, university lecturers, airhostess, engineers, bankers, reporters, pilots, architects, designers and etc. modernization they call it.

So, why does Dinka society still hold on to harmful cultural economic views about girl child? Why do parents seem to still attach their futuristic prosperity to their daughters? Below are various forms of grave dangers related to bride wealth and the matrimonial abuses a girl faces:

Bride Price: Bride wealth, mostly in form of cattle, is part of what makes Dinka people. It has been practiced since time immemorial. Without cows, a man cannot get married to any girl. This makes cattle more valuable than any other thing amongst many communities in South Sudan. This 'highly-valuedness' of cattle bears a number of complex problems.

One of them is cattle rustling. Yes this practice is as old as the Nile River. But since the 1980s, characterized with conflict – civil war, the demand for cows has been rising. In the conflict, many animals were killed in aerial attacks on cattle camps by Khartoum government forces.

Others (bulls) were given to the Anya-anya/SPLA as voluntary taxes by civilians. This move was a symbol of solidarity with the freedom fighters. Some villagers were robbed of their cows at gunpoint by the SPLA though.

Other communities resorted to killing their animals for food after prolonged droughts and famines. Many animals also died from various livestock diseases. As a result, intensified cattle raiding became the order of the day because young men had/have to take their girlfriends home as wives.

Another troublous string attached to bride wealth is death: To drive off cattle, a raider must first attack and kill the owner who is equally armed. The owner loses both cattle and his life. This gives birth to retaliatory attacks, tribal wars and inability to coexist.

It is also against the government's compulsory school policy. Many parents rather send their children to cattle camps where they look after livestock.

High Bride Price: This is highly detrimental to economy today. After meeting such a mountain of demand, some young families end up with nothing. In fact, many grooms are forced to borrow from relatives to complete payment of bride price. Raising the first child becomes a challenge. They struggle again to stand on their feet. A newly wed gentle is reduced to beggary- a clean suits-and-tie pauper.

Connubial Servitude: These profligate marriages seem to make men assume absolute power over their spouses. With majority of South Sudanese women and girls dangerously uncivilized, they easily conform to the prejudicial multi-millennium old practice.

Men treat women as they wish. And any resistance offered by their wives is met with "Shut up, I paid several cows on your head. Get back to the kitchen." They never get involved in important family issues that require decision making. They are simply statuettes. They become housewives – pure baby-making machines.

Negative Polygamy: Again, since men are everything - sole providers of life, they feel they can bring in an "Adeujok or Ng'eudek" anytime. Or others just grab teenage girls so long as they can mute their parents. Thanks to wealth. Sadly, the best game ever played by two or more housewives is he-loves-me-more-than-he-loves-you game. They fight over scarce resources or nothing, almost every day. They end up baptizing one another with over-boiled water.

What I find annoyingly contradictory is that, though a bride fetches lots of cows in marriage, she, in many ways, continues to support her mother and father and siblings forever.

In conclusion, I think the best thing, the only best thing ever, any South Sudanese father, particularly a Dinka and Nuer, can do to his daughter today is take his economic eyes off her and concentrate on her education. School her. An educated girl is 'unmistreatable.' She develops strengths of all kinds – soul, mind, personality. She gains many freedoms too, especially financial independence. Remember over-dependence on husbands is the very reason why illiterate women subscribe to matrimonial enslavement. Love and nothing but love is the force which holds today's couple together. Not money. Not cows.

However, taking economic eyes off girls should not give any single daughter any reason to run around with retarded youth in nightclubs.

My Unseen Tears as a Lost Boy

September 17, 2013

Two days before my departure, my uncle summoned me. I found him seated in his compound, under huge achui'il tree. Also present were my other uncles and some clan elders. Seated on a mat, on the other side of the shade were my aunts, grandmother, mother and many other clannish women.

I sat on a bench next to my cousins who had to squeeze harder to create a space for me. Though I did not know what the summoning was all about, I felt it was a lecture – a life-time briefing about how they wished I would handle myself in a distant land.

And of course I was right. "In two days, you will no longer be with us," junior Uncle James introduced the agenda, "you are going to Amirka, the White man's land."

When each and every elder said whatever they wanted to say to me, my uncle, Deng, 60, who happens to be my father's elder brother, began to speak: "My nephew, I have nothing much to tell you but just to remind you of the reason why you had to leave your ancestral home in the late 1980s. Remember what John Garang thinks of you. Remember why he took you away from the cattle camps. He had a dream, a big one. He pictured that after war, there would be a new breed of leaders, educated ones, a new race whose duty is to continue from where freedom fighters will end the struggle. That dream is you. You and the rest of the boys are the seeds of our country. So, go to Amirka. Do nothing else but acquire knowledge. Go to school. Get all the academic papers there are on earth."

Before the meeting came to an end, my grandma got up and walked over to me and spat saliva on my head. To spit particles of saliva on a young person's head signifies blessing in my culture. "You've heard what your uncles just said," she added. "Go and don't you ever forget where you come from."

A week later, I arrived in the United States of America - in a small town called Lubbock, Texas. My first days in here were trying, very rough. The cold weather, the strange foods, the half-naked and wild girls, and everything that was new to me - my body. Anyway, days turned into weeks and weeks turned into months. I got used to the new place quickly though.

Thinking about the horrifying situation my family, extended, was living in in the camp, I felt like helping them. No, I was obligated to do so. I sent them a few hundreds of dollars I had saved during my first months here. With their conditions in mind, I kept sending them little money from time to time. However, one day, I thought about what they told me shortly before I left them. I framed a plan. I sketched the way forward. After about two months, I rang my Uncle Deng.

"I enrolled in school yesterday, Uncle," I said. "That means I will no longer be sending you the little like usual. For now, I've sent you a thousand dollars. I know it's not much but I hope it will help you and the family."

Uncle Deng took my position positively and encouraged me. He reiterated the significance of education.

After our conversation, I had my telephone line disconnected. And I concentrated on my studies – first semester, second semester and third semester. Here, my distant cousin told my schoolmate to tell me that my uncle wanted to talk to me, that I should ring him up immediately. The messenger handed me a piece of paper, with digits scribbled on it.

My heart raced. Though I could not figure out what the matter was, something told me that something terrible must have gone wrong back in the camp. I was disturbed so much. It was during a short break when I received the message. I returned to class but I don't thing I really paid attention. I was so disturbed. Everything looked blurry in the classroom. I remember only seeing my lecturer moving his lips up and down. Poor me!

When I phoned Uncle a couple of hours later, I learned that there was no problem at all only that 'life was getting worse' in the camp. I believed him. But I did not have money. I was broke, an educatee. So, I borrowed some money from a friend who agreed to my request on condition that I would pay him back in ten days. That week, I worked my ass off, doing an unspeakable menial job to refund the dude.

In the weeks that followed, we had another lengthy conversation with Uncle. It was about life. The convo was interesting until he 'slapped it in the ear'. He suggested that I get married. "Your peers are getting married," his voice tinged with marital territorial aggression. "They're paying millions of shillings on heads of beautiful girls back here......son of Maduldit is here in Africa to wed. He managed to make a lot of dollars so fast. Why not you?"

Dang! I couldn't believe my ears. The same old uncle who advised me to study hard to become a lawyer or doctor was telling me to drop my academic dreams for marriage? "What about school, Uncle?"

He convincingly said many things about our lineage – how we have always stood out in the community - that we've never been looked down upon by any family before. "Now is the time to remind them of who we are. Do you remember the youngest daughter of Mayomdit? – That light-skinned sweet little girl who used to play with Atoch? She has grown to be the most beautiful girl in the neighborhood. Many lost-boys have shown interest in her. However, Mayomdit says he will affiance her to any suitor who offers more wealth. Don't let us down, son."

Dear reader, what would your reaction have been if you were me? Well, here we go. I redrew my life-path. And that is work and school. I began to juggle books and money. I worked at night and attended day classes.

After I raised enough money, I gave uncle a green light to talk to Mayomdit about the proposal. Prior to that, I had delegated my cousins to be intermediates. As my culture allows, they talked to the girl on my behalf. They conducted a successful love campaign for me.

I eventually went back to the camp where I spent three months, undergoing wedding preparations. Mayomdit and his wife favorably responded to my request. I was among the five suitors who sought his permission to take his daughter as wife. I presented 2,000,000 KES in cash plus 40 heads of cattle which were to be given to him in Bor. Down the aisle, I walked my gorgeous bride, Ayen, in 2007.

Before I returned to the US, I opted to rent a house in Komarock, Nairobi. My newly-wedded wife and my younger siblings moved in. Her siblings and mum joined them a year later. An army of relatives, isn't it? All this – my new marital status and the house in Komarock - changed me. I became more selfless. I became more and more drawn to work than school.

I made sure that my family did not suffer. I paid for their school fees. When I took up the responsibility, some were in primary school and others, secondary. As you read this sentence, three of them are graduating early next year and others are taking short diploma programs in various Nairobi colleges. And my firstborn son is a 2nd grader. The last one is yet to go to school.

With all I have done, with all the unconditional and altruistic sacrifices I have offered, with all the uprightness I have shown my community, I hear people, my own people, talk bad of me. They say really bad things about me and my kind. They shoot demeaning questions randomly.

They ask why I am still in school. "By the way, when is your brother completing his Bachelor's Degree?" a relative asked my little brother the other day. "Is he really at school or sipping margaritas with blonde broads in America?"

Annoyingly enough, my Uncle, the same man who drove

educational nail into my head, unbelievably told me on phone recently that he doesn't understand 'what is keeping me in Amirka' yet my peers, the ones I went to the US with, are now back in South Sudan where they are deploying sophisticated expertise they acquired from American schools.

Worse of all, I'm not in good terms with my wife right now. With the monthly family up-keeps I send her, she started drinking alcohol after giving birth to my second child. Her friends in Nairobi influenced her. She openly goes out every weekend with her friends, single ladies.

When I ask why, she says: "These are modern times, dude. It's my life, my choice. You either bear with it or do whatever you wanna do, man." Can you believe that?

I am not alone though. My friends who exclusively got engaged in studies during their early years in the US say they are also receiving such blind complaints from members of their communities. "All your peers are married, with children," flies a concern, "What have you been doing in Amirka? When are you getting married, mathon? You're aging."

My Uncle

April 23, 2012

YOU JUST OFFERED ME YOUR OLD V-8 AND CREDITED MY BANK account with a huge amount of dollars but I don't think that will stop me from speaking my mind. There's something that I have been keeping to myself, something that I have always wanted to tell you, something that disturbs me, something my peers abhor you for. I defend you though. It is high time now I tell you in this short note. It's going to be disheartening, however, close your eyes and take a deep breath before you proceed to the next paragraph.

Here we go… it's both ironical and incomprehensible how our grandfathers, fathers, aunts, friends, mothers, sisters and even yourself bled, sweated and shed tears, sacrificially, for more than a century in a quest to detach south Sudanese from the claws of Islamic rule yet you still dumbly ignorantly selfishly plug us in the socket of Arab world by indecisively rushing to their states in order to attract investments, given the hidden agenda that comes with their development proposals.

An Arab is an Arab; be he a sheikh, politician, hawker or shopkeeper. His mission is one and simple; to Arabize and Islamize everyone, anywhere. I don't think you need a PhD in History to trace back how they came and the price of their presence in Sudan, of which we have paid dearly. Even your seven-year son Nomedij can recite it before an international audience. An Arab always strives to change you, in and out; from names, color of skin, lifestyle, name it. You ask the people of Nuba Mountains.

Let me take you back a little bit by elaborating how ungrateful ingrates these folks are. Back in the day, the Arabs came to Sudan as single male merchants. I repeat; single male merchants. They arrived and settled in Khartoum, an area allegedly inhabited by Dinka people. That was before the cleverer race invented the Calendar. As they carried on with their businesses, and after they showered the unsuspecting Dinka chiefs and elders with gifts of mirrors, sweets, salt and soaps, they requested the old dudes for a number of things.

First of all, they asked for pieces of land for erecting shops. And then they asked for girls for marriage, a request I suspect the sly Dinka people gladly assented to since they felt it was the best way to rid of their ugly, promiscuous and lazy daughters. Remember, today's Dinka folks practice that business. They marry off our unmarriageable sisters to foreigners. Doesn't that remind you of what happened the other day?

Anyway, the girl-sweet-salt-business continued as long as the first guys found it lucrative. They invited over their brothers, uncles and friends back home to join them. They eventually multiplied and started showing their true colors – master-like behaviors. They began to control everything, both that moved and that didn't. They did a lot with the natives.

They sold some into slavery and made some laborers. But with the inability of cattle-rearing communities to succumb to change easily, the Dinka waged countless wars against their nieces but lost, forcing them to migrate to different parts of Sudan. See? Northerners are our biological nieces because their existence is as a result of the aforementioned unions. I understand the Dinka were so arrogant, some still are, such that a slave would turn away leftovers, claiming that he should have partaken in the meals at the table with his master's family. Since then, the feud rages on.

Now, wasn't it yesterday that the Nile River overflowed with blood and bodies of innocent women and children that were ceremoniously slaughtered by Arabs just because they refused to be Arabic? Or has it been too long to remember the root cause of the 21-year civil war that claimed 2.5 million lives and displaced 4 million more, including your children?

Then, what on earth makes you travel to their cities to lobby investments from their companies, or attain capacity-building there? Who has bewitched you, uncle? Does South Sudan have to attract investments from the Middle East? What world records have they set or broken in terms of development apart from high unemployment rates, low wages and widespread stinking poverty?

Or do you have shares in the Arab companies you bring into the baby country? In fact, rumors say so. I will stop here because I feel the few remarks will brainstorm you.

One more thing though, I want you to talk to your daughter; the one who calls herself Lady Gaga. Lately she has been drinking a lot with friends. Most of them broke. I doubt she attends her classes regularly. Haven't you been wondering why she keeps asking you for more money? Apparently, she is an ATM machine. There's this broke boyfriend of hers who has assumed the nature of a tick. The guy clings to her so badly.

She pays his rent, buys him pants. I tried to talk her out of her brand new lifestyle but she instead hailed insults at me, calling me names. Furthermore, she doesn't wear enough clothes nowadays. The first thing you see when she appears is her breasts. They hang, naked; with only the nipples covered. When asked why, she says our grandmas used to wear nothing at all. "So, why disturb someone who has at least dressed?" She asks. The next thing to worry about her dress code is her skirts. They are too short. You can see her underwear even when she is standing! And she calls anyone who dares rebuke her, uncivilized.

You must be wondering why I haven't deposited all the money into your foreign bank account. It's because the bank manager, on seeing stacks of dollars, and especially after I failed to account for the source, threatened to call cops on me. I lied to him that it was for a registered company based in Juba. He instructed me to get proper papers in order to bank the notes, and that was after I bribed him heavily. I have resorted to banking the money in bits and pieces just to avoid possible interrogations by Interpol. I will have banked it all by June this year. If I may ask, where did you get this large sum from, uncle?

I almost forgot. I'm obliged to educate you about your concubine. Forgive my language. I would have used a better or at least mannerly reference had the English people created a polite word for concubine.

She is playing you. I mean, she fakes her love for you, believe it or not. Worst of all, the baby is not yours. The father of the baby is an old boyfriend who she broke up with after she conceived. I learned that the dude disowned her because he didn't have what it takes to feed extra mouths; but he resurfaced when he realized she is alive and kicking.

Thanks to your unsuspectingness. Or is it negligence? You may find it hard to believe this: I, for no specific reason, tampered with her phone while she was in the kitchen. I entered into the "sent items" folder where I found an SMS that she sent. It reads "Dear sweetheart, there's no reason you should doubt my forgiveness. I told you last time that I do understand why you refused to take responsibility for my pregnancy. You were a student and had no money. Besides, the baby is yours…… I love you and want you so bad. The old fool left for Juba this morning, come home tonight and correct what the old man doesn't do right…"

Bleaching is Self-Destruction

February 20, 2013

IT IS INARGUABLE THAT GIRLS OR WOMEN WHO BLEACH SKIN ARE THOSE that are suffering from low self-esteem. They are cheap. So cheap.

Cheap females are those who always want to please every man, any man. Frog man. Hyena man. They always want to be said to be beautiful even when they are not. They flash a smile at any man, any time. Anywhere.

They are gullible. The word NO does not exist in their dictionary. They take anything placed before them. They don't question; they never scrutinize. That is why they believe that, to be considered beautiful, one must be light-skinned or purely white.

They are not contented with what they are, who they are. If you are not comfortable in your own skin, if you don't appreciate the skin color the creator gave you, one of the elements you are identified with - to an extent of arming yourself with chemicals to terrorize it, then you are insane. You're sick. Seek a psychiatrist.

It is an indirect message that you are a trash, a bin. Anybody can use you as a dump site. You lose respect.

Be informed, beauty is never determined by the color of skin. What counts is the physique; face, eye size, legs, waist, dental formula, mouth size, etc. You may be as white as an Irish but if you have feet that look like those of a goat and a face that looks like a chicken's, never shall you be seen as beautiful. Never.

"Skin terrorists" may not be prostitutes in your city but in mine, they are. My city is Juba. Wherever they come from, whatever school they went to in Kenya, Uganda, Sudan or Egypt, the school motto must have been "Bleach, Attract Men, Make Money." Nothing else.

I am not referring to nationals of the aforementioned countries; I am talking about South Sudanese young girls, prostitutes. Let's call them Lolitas.

In school, they never took learning seriously. They were there for prestige, for fun. "Oh I am in St. this. Oh I'm in St. that." That's it. All they focused on was boy-girl relationship. They spent most of their time practicing the contents of Mexican soap operas.

After four years of doing nothing in high school, they graduate with Es. Some do not even graduate. They just drop out.

While at home (Eldoret, Nakuru, Nairobi, Kampala. Etc), they hear of interesting stories about Juba. They begin to understand the meaning of a diva, the importance of financial independence - independent woman.

They get to know about "mur-dih." Murdih is Dinka for birth canal. In this context, it means a car. A car gotten through sex money.

After getting all these ideas, they move to Juba where they launch "Operation Buy Mur-dih." OBM in short. It involves a lot of things. Name change is the first thing they put into practice. Followed by skin lightening. The looks of other body organs are also changed, temporarily.

Let's talk about breasts. After years of playing sex game with niggas, the chest becomes flat again. They are called folded chapattis. And to attract those rich sex maniacs in Juba, a girl resorts to redesigning her bust. She manages that with the help of sponge and bra. She pushes those useless boobs up the throat, making breathing difficult. She be choking herself. That's why when she finally arrives in her Tukul during wee morning hours, she unties the load and says, under her breath: "Uh thank you, Lord. At least I can breathe again, with ease."

The name change idea is aimed at confusing men. Today, she introduces herself as Angelina Jolie. Tomorrow she is Nicki Minaj. Yesterday she was Keyshia Cole.

You should see them in night clubs hunting men, stalking them. From one social place to another, they move in groups of twos or threes. You barely see them remove cash from their handbags. I don't know why but I think they never have enough money to spend on drinks as they spend the little they get on hairdo, foods and cosmetics.

The smart ones do not roam the night aimlessly; they await deals from rich men who call them up to show up in private posh hotel rooms in town.

The other group which comprises of woman - single mothers - gatecrashes big government functions, cocktail parties. You can never fail to notice them. They are the loud ones. With "Bakur" smeared all over the body, one can never part without asking for her number. That scent is so tempting, brother.

Besides the self-degrading act, apart from the mental slavery they portray, bleaching brings about a lot of side effects. It weakens the skin. It makes it vulnerable to a number of first class diseases. Cancer tops the list. You know what that means.

According to medical research, skin terrorists also develop increased appetite. Just imagine that. Who would want to get married to an avaricious girl? A gluttonous food-loving woman in this bad economy? The one who goes to KFC and buys chicken in bulk, goes home and eats it up in the bedroom?

Bareness is another side effect of bleaching. How many barren young women do you know of today? – A lot, I guess. Try and memorize if they ever used creams.

Finally, bleaching could be another way of supporting science projects run by inhumane greedy. Look, one man manufactures the cream. A woman buys and uses it. After some times, the cream gives birth to cancer. Then another man goes on TV and says he's got the cure for cancer. Now, you move from hospital to hospital looking for affordable drugs. All you do is buying. Do you see the trap you get yourself into?

No
to Foreign Religions

NHIALIC, YOU KNOW ME VERY WELL. I DON'T COMPLAIN A LOT. YOU created me. I appreciate who I am and what I have. I accept anything that comes my way just the way it is or I work out a few modifications at least to suit my taste, without bugging people close to me. I sometimes simply change my attitude whenever I find a problem too hard to cope with.

That's how I have been surviving this unforgiving world for the past twenty-something years. But now I am afraid, I have failed to tackle something, something that is increasingly attacking my originality. And that's why I am presenting it to you, as my creator, to look into it seriously. It is this thing called religion.

Remember I was born into a Dinka family. Dinka people are religious souls, naturally. They believe in two divine bodies; you, Nhialic and Jok. We believe in life after death. According to Dinka mythology, you are the creator of everything, including our cows. You are all-powerful and the controller of all events. You prohibit and condemn wrong-doings of any kinds. You hate dishonesty, stealing, killing, adultery, lying, disobedience, name it. You encourage love, peace and harmony amongst brothers and sisters.

You also love good neighborliness. You, who normally appear to us through parents, write down your expectations in every Dinka fetus' essence, of which the parents help instill into the child through upbringing. That's why Dinka parents beat their children thoroughly whenever they go astray. Frankly, you don't have to be the parent to spank a Dinka brat. Anyone can beat the cream out of it provided that you caught the young rascal misbehaving.

Jok is more of your opposite. He is some greedy super being that talks to its followers through signs and sorcerers or magicians. He is in form of python, turtle, cobra or monitor lizard, depending which clan. He angrily and violently reacts when annoyed. He demands for bulls to be slaughtered to appease him.

What one worships depends on a family or clan. For me, my great parents were followers of you, Nhialic, until some strange, pale-skinned, tall, aged creatures with bushy faces and long big knob-like noses showed up in my motherland about two hundred years ago. They settled and quickly began to preach the contents of a big black book that is white inside.

The book, popularly known as Bible, condemns everything Dinka, you in particular. Those who believe in biblical teachings are called Christians. Christianity attacks your divinity, claiming you're a false super being and places the white man's first. The bible calls him God. I have read the bible several times, cover to cover. It talks about the same things you planted in me - knowing right and wrong.

Bible was written by some crooked sneaky white people who, I feel, deleted and or added some valuable information. It is supposed to be a history book just like any other book that talks about the past. I don't hold any grudge against Christians and their bible but the problem sets in when they consider my beliefs uncouth and unacceptable, and try by all means necessary to have me believe in theirs. There's nothing they like about me.

They want me to change the way I am; what I am called, way of life, what I believe in and so on. Whenever I introduce myself as Ayuen, everyone rolls on the ground laughing. They suggest Jewish names like Jeroboam, Ecclesiastes, Ananias or Maccabees, of which I find unreasonable since they hold no substance to my lineage. They say my identity sucks. They use the biblical passages to force me into accepting their ways. They talk about some place called hell - that if I don't believe in their super being, I will go to hell. Where the hell is hell?

One thing that makes it hard for me to believe them is the bible itself. Its contents do not refer to me as a Dinka in anyway. Take for example the first commandment in which their God threatens, "I am the Lord your God, who brought you out of the land of Egypt, out of the house of bondage. You shall have no other gods before me." How the hell does that concern me? I am a Dinka, a cattle rustler by birth. Have the Dinka people ever been in Egypt? If yes, then they must have been the ones who enslaved God's people, and not the ones told to worship one God.

Another reason why I reject their ways is that they don't practice what they preach: "Thou shalt not make unto thee any graven image, or any likeness of anything that is in heaven above, or that is in the earth beneath, or that is in the water under the earth." See? Their God prohibits them from making idols, a command they defiantly urinate on by embracing this thing called cross which is worn on the neck. Some carry larger cumbersome wooden crosses. I heard that cross was used by romans to kill their holy ghost's son. What if the son was shot between the eyes, would they be wearing bullets on their necks?

Homosexuality issue is another thing that makes me question the reality and trueness of their religion. Leviticus chapter 18 verse 22-23 says "You shall not lie with a male as one lies with a female; it is an abomination." yet the world's largest church, catholic, supports it. A 2011 report compiled by the Washington DC-based Public Religion Research Institute, using past polls and studies showed that nearly three-quarters of Catholics favor either allowing gay and lesbian people to marry (43%) or allowing them to form civil unions (31%). Only 22% of Catholics say there should be no legal recognition of a gay couple's relationship.

Recently, the UK Prime Minister in an interview with BBC was said to have threatened to cut aid to anti-gay countries, stating that countries receiving UK support should adhere to proper human rights. What human rights? If human rights give criminals absolute immunity to punishment, what do you expect murderers to say? Form their associations that would present their issues in the parliament? Where is the credibility of what they believe in? Do I really need to believe them?

A number of big church elders indulge in a lot of bad practices. They sleep around with married female members of the congregations. Somewhere in my current location in 2010, a married pastor was caught red-handed, making love to a policeman's woman. Community members offered him neither mercy nor grace, especially because he was heard preaching against adultery in a crusade the day before. They beat them both, stripped them naked and forced them to kiss in public. See? And how many cases of that kind go unnoticed? Thousands!

Wait, there is more. In July, 2007, A Zimbabwe's state-controlled television broadcast photographs showing Archbishop X in bed with a married woman. The woman's husband later filed a lawsuit that sought about $80,000. How about this thing called "vow of celibacy?" what happened to it?

Somewhere in the bible, the whole mankind traces its way back to two first beings; Adam and Eve. Where did their sons, Cain and Abel, find girls they got married to? How did that happen? Bible does not say.

These people called believers never cease to make me smile. They do things just to show off superiority. A bunch of those who are tired of doing big bad things spent months, begging and kissing another arrogant group to not launch a dangerous missile into the orbit. They defiantly held their middle fingers up high and launched the rocket, but failed due to some unknown reasons. Maybe you were behind their failure. Weren't you, Nhialic?

They manufacture guns and distribute them to hostile communities who attack the peaceful ones for fun. Indeed, people can neither defend themselves nor their livestocks from these unfriendly neighbors who now use sophisticated weapons like RPGs and rocket launchers to attack and drive away the cattle you gave us. But quickly they go on radio and television, condemning their very acts. Thanks to their gods.

All the same, they nicknamed me pagan, atheist, non-believer, infidel and so on. There is another religion whose male believers tie white turban around the head and they keep long tidy beards. One of their celebrated men was shot down by a tall black guy in 2011. They are also trying harder to talk me into becoming one of their own. My female workmate provocatively calls me kafir, meaning an unbeliever. She dresses up like a ninja. I hardly see her face. I fight back by telling her that her face is either too ugly to show or she has a big wound on her head or she can't afford to pay a hairdresser.

Now, why are they telling me to leave you and worship theirs? Is it because I am black? Or are you inferior to their gods? They have managed to convert my brothers and sisters though, particularly the older ones. I call them religious slaves because they got cheated or misled. They go to church Monday to Monday, when they should be working, farming.

The book of Titus says "Our people must learn to devote themselves to doing what is good, in order that they may provide for daily necessities and not live unproductive lives." The owners of the religion they abandoned theirs for work hard and go to club every day and go to church maybe once a year. Do you feel me, Nhialic?

In my third-eye perspective, since bible scriptures directly refer to Israelis, then it was meant to be the national constitution for Israelis, and holy Koran for Iraqis. I have my own laws outlined in a book called National Transitional Constitution of South Sudan. The constitution adds nothing other than annotates the moral grammar you wired into my neural circuits by evolution.

It is evident that Africa is the place where world super powers show off their influences. During the past centuries, they greedily scrambled and partitioned it with intent to suck her resources dry, of which they did. That was an economical competition. A religious one followed. Old men preached word of their gods which condemned African ways, while their sons pleasurably enslaved, raped, killed and sold Africans. Nothing much has changed today; same song, different verse.

These people are so hypocritical. They condemn corrupt, thieving African politicians while on the other hand helping them hide stolen billions of dollars in their banks, leaving the ordinary men with nothing but protruding ribs. Others grant asylum to African butchers, the committers of genocidal actions. What's biblical about that? Nothing!

So, why do they speak against wrong-doing in their big black books but offer first class protection mechanisms to the wrong-doers? Whose beliefs are worth rebuking? And who should abandon his and adore the others'? Who is better off?

PART III

POEMS

The Son

Look,
You broke ass son of a hunter
Do you know who you're messing with?
Do you have an idea who the fuck I am?
You seem to know nothing about me, uh?
Okay, listen
I am the son of the president
Did you hear that?
My dad is the president
Read my lips, preee-ssssi-denn-t
We run this country

We rule you, motherfucker
We own everything in it;
The airport, the police, the army, the rivers and
    mountains, the wildlife,
The oil, the banks, the hospitals, the media, the
    mountains,
The roads, the whole city
Everything
Even yourself!
We own you and your poor parents
We've got your lives in the palms of our hands
We decide who lives and who dies
That's our responsibility,
Our mandate
It's written
We can raise taxes,
Quadruple food prices,
Ban imports,
And hoard basic food items like flour,
Sugar, bread and milk
If we like,
Just to cleanse the country of roaches like you
I could call my dad right now to instruct his boys to do it
And believe me, by the end of six months,
You would have starved to death
As a wild fire consumes savannah grassland in summer,
So would hunger and diseases feast on your siblings
Or there are so many ways to kill a rat
We could just shut all the windows of survival,
With exception of only one
Guess what it is

It's your sister, fool
We could mold her into something else,
An idol
Something monetary,
A sex trade commodity
We could turn her into a hawker,
A professional prostitute,
Who would satisfy my dad's business friends' sexual
    adventures
Imagine how much she would be getting in exchange of
    her body
With only one source of income, you people wouldn't
    die quickly though
But slowly and painfully,
Both physically and emotionally

So, what makes you think I can't enter this club with my
    Nine?
Like I told you earlier,
We own everything
This nightclub is also my dad's
I have access to it,
Anytime,
Any day,
Whether I am carrying an RPG or 50 Cal
It's none of your fucking business
Now get the fuck out of my way,
Before I put a bullet in your dumb head
And have your body dumped in the river
I said get the fuck out of my way!
Okay,

You have the guts to push me, uh?
I see
You are planning to commit a suicide, right?
Dude, I won't let you do that
Coz you are already dead,
Half-dead
Poverty killed your other half
And it is about to take away the remaining half
In fact, you were born like that – half-dead,
Half-human being
Fully poor
A son of a pauper
Thanks to your uncle, Grinding Poverty!
The only blood brother of your father
And now you want me to stain my hands with your
     stinking blood?
Hell no
No way!
I am not going to waste my bullet on a worthless thing
     like you
I would rather shoot a dog or a baboon

Yes I am a drunkard and so what?
What do you expect of a big boy like me,
A big boy whose father is the most powerful man
     around here?
We got all the money, man
In my house, we do not use toilet rolls
Toilet paper is a symbol of poverty
It indicates how poor one is
I tell you,

In my place, we wipe our asses with dollar bills,
Hundreds, to be specific
So, what comes to your mind?
All I do is drink,
Smoke weed, shisha, cigars and cigarettes,
F@%k,
Eat,
And sleep
So, how does my drinking concern you?
Or are you jealous of the liquor brand I am drinking?
Dude, this is called Cognac
I believe you can't pronounce that, Mister Never-Been-
      To-School
Now read my lips again, ko-ni-ak
Cognac is a French brandy, fool
You have never tasted it,
And never shall you taste it
It's very expensive, dude
It would cost you one of your kidneys to buy a cognac,
You broke ass motherfucker
I don't even know why I am talking to you,
You knucklehead

What?
What do you mean, get a life?
Do I look like I got no life?
Look me in the eye
Check me out,
From my toes to the head;
My designer jeans, my UGG boots, my Heuer Carrera,
My dreadlocks, my tattoos, my iPhone, my drawers

Now tell me,
What life are you talking about?
I ride a Chrysler 300 C
I own two mansions,
One in Kampala, one in Nairobi,
Another in Sydney
I got millions of dollars in the bank
Isn't that life?
I have been to many places,
Cities you have never dreamt of
I have been to Havana, Dublin, Oslo, Rio de Janeiro,
Jamaica, Buenos Aires, Atlanta, Lagos and Antananarivo,
To mention but just a few
If it is about school,
Forget it, man
Yes I discontinued my studies
Because I saw no reason of learning
In fact, I shouldn't have enrolled in school in the first
    place
School is for poor dudes like you
A vehicle for escaping beggary,
A means of keeping wretchedness at bay

For me, my destiny is set
From day one,
The very day I was planted in my mum's womb
Like father like son,
In few years coming, I will be the president
Yes, I am a prospective Commander-in-Chief of armed
    forces,
The would-be controller of everything in this country

The heir of my father's business empire
The inheritor of this country
And remember I don't need scholastic crap to rule you
The fact that my father was once the president is enough
It mandates my future presidency
Automatically, it gives me all the qualities of a leader
Even if I don't succeed my father,
I will succeed one of his protégés
Shortly before the end of his tenure,
Dad's protégé will visit us in our family house
He will explain to mum and my uncles his intentions,
That it is about time I am groomed for presidency

Shut the f up!
And put that fake phone away
Let me finish
Yes, we will all welcome the good news
Immediately, we won't wait to celebrate,
To pop bottles of champagne
This would bring my drinking,
And my smoking to a pause,
As I concentrate on the campaign trails
With my father known as a hero,
The former president,
The man of the people
It would not take that long to win voters' admirations
The paupers who take pride in names,
Things that are devoid of meaning
Folks who scramble to submit in their votes for my
        presidential candidacy
With the sole hope of being rewarded with the crumbs,

That fall off the table,
Hope that never materializes
By the way, this is the only time you're considered
     valuable
During elections, we value you
You become a valuable customer,
A political customer
All we require from you is a vote
Nothing else
After that, we forget your ass until another election
     season
That's how we do it
We, the born to rule

Hey!
Who the hell are you people?
Let go of my arms
Stop pulling me
Shit!
What?
So you are cops, uh?
So, this filthy dude called cops on me?
I see
And you idiots got the balls to lay your hands on me?
Silly smelly cops
You little rats,
You just got your asses fired
That, I promise you
Wait till my dad learns of this.......

True Patriot

By everything,
I am a citizen of this country
My government is what I am allegiant to
Its citizens too
Amongst them are my kids, wife,
 Father, mother, brothers and sisters
Like any other citizen, I have a responsibility
Practically, I protect and preserve the sovereignty of my
    birthplace
My cause is simple
It is a matter of life and death;
I spill blood
Blood of he who disrespects my country
Blood of he who dares to call me an insect

I shoot the bastard between the eyes
Blaow!!
Or I just sink my bayonet deep into his chest
Strip him of his shiny boots and
Jerbania and belt
Leaving the son of a bitch writhing
His ass leaking with dung, human's
When fighting pauses
I trudge to my base, weak and starving
I took my last meals seven days ago
But it's okay coz I am used to no food
I eat irregularly
I am waifish, malnourished;
Physically weak
But I consider it temporary weakness
Because whenever a warfare erupts
The weakness flies away,
Leaving a sinewy triggerman
That's what I was raised to be
Look:
When I was in mum's womb
I could hear the sound of gunshots
My mother shook my head
As she ran helter-skelter
For our dear lives
At two or so
I saw what was going down with my own eyes
I could see my people felled like trees
I saw houses burn to ashes
At six, instead of learning a-e-i-o-u
I chose something else

Ak-47
I learnt how to fire the shit
As you can tell
My career is about heads
I simply blow them off
During the long engagement
I stayed loyal
I obeyed every command barked at me
By my superiors
With empty stomach
I attacked, captured, liberated towns
I was ever in frontline
While my bloods rotted in refugee camps
Got eaten alive by starvation
Yet those of my superiors
Lived, schooled in foreign neighboring towns
As they got fattened by their mums
That frequently received dollars
My comrades and I were promised
Good life after the civil war
What happened to the promises?
Or did they die along with Garang?
The guys above seem to be celebrating success
They are adding weight day by day
They are now fat-necks
I feel duped, fooled, cheated, and lied to
The truth of the matter is
I subsist on mango fruits, ripe ones
I survive on grass too, sometimes
Not because I like grass
But because the situation dictates it

Yes I get remunerations
Very inadequate
My learned cousins call it peanuts
Tripling it would not help
I am married, with kids
I can't describe the situation
My family faces
Coz I don't want to make you cry
For the love of my country
That outweighs everything else
I won't do anything stupid a disgruntled soldier does
I can't complain either
Coz only the infirm complain
I will soldier on, with dignity
Until my death gives me a call
Remember, as you take your meals today,
I, your defender, still live on mango

CDF Thief

I'm an MP, an elected MP
Constitutionally, I represent my people
I'm their spokesperson
I raise their issues
I'm a law-maker,
An examiner of the work of the government
I check out how it spends taxes raised by my people
I contribute to debates on national issues
I receive Constituency Development Funds,
I'm in charge of how and what to spend it on
As its name suggests,

The sum is meant for development,
For the betterment of my constituents' lives
It's usually a large amount
For building healthcare centers,
Strengthening security,
Establishing schools
Building road networks to connect my constituency
With its neighboring areas

I'm an MP, an elected MP
I know that
Whenever a constituency has good road networks,
Better health clinics and schools for children to go to-
Or in short, if I spend the CDF well:
Workers work;
Nurses nurse
Traders trade
Teachers teach
Farmers farm
They gather good harvests
Granaries get filled up
Everyone eats enough food
Starvation emigrates
Men take pride in their brand new pot-bellies
Women develop big buttocks,
Just like my wives'
Surpluses are sold
 Local trade flourishes
She winks and purrs
And beckons to the private sector
Investors come kneeling, begging

Factories mushroom
Smoke emitted by manufacturing
Companies is seen afar off
As you approach my small town
Employment opportunities call my people out
By their nicknames:
"Marvis, Poni, Asidih, Gatluak, Ukel, Wani
Come and work here. Please don't turn down this
   chance
It comes with a lot of benefits;
Medical cover for you and your family, car, house
   allowances,
Free scholarships for your children up to university"
No doubt,
Living standards improve
Every face wears an infectious smile
Only few fall sick
Mothers give birth safely,
To bouncing babies
Infant mortality goes on leave, permanent leave
Maternal mortality hits the road
Girls and boys go to school
They study uninterrupted
Before leaving campus;
Some become athletes, international footballers,
Singers, dunkers
They graduate
As doctors, bankers, geologists, environmentalists
They work for international organizations
The likes of ICC and the World Bank
The cycle is broken,

A new page is turned;
No more cattle rustlers
Violent crime rate drops
Bandits confess and repent
Child abduction disappears
Forced marriage becomes history
Ethnic hostilities go missing
But who cares about the CDF anyway?
Who amongst my subjects knows what it is for?
Who knows when it is released?
Who knows how much?
Who follows it up?
Who knows when the last one was released?
Did anyone question me
Over its spending?
Does anybody really bother to know whether I'm
      actually engaged in
Any of the projects I propose?
The ones I get approvals from the parliament?
Could it be journalist?
This country's reporters?
Ha ha ha ha ha ha
Do they really know anything?
I don't think they are typical reporters
What do they know?
I do watch them
 No passion
No interest
I think majority are in the media business
Because it's the only job that has presented itself to them
Only few try though

None of them has ever unearthed
Any of the greatest scandals my comrades and I commit
I think they just bluff,
Pretending to be rough and tough
There's a one boy-journalist that wears dreadlocks
I do spot him during official functions
And in the streets collecting vox pops
He wears his pants below the waist
Traditionally, journalists are official enemies for folks
      like me
They are snoopers
But can this one, the pant-sagging type be of any harm?
Does he have what it takes to watch out for?
I don't think so!

I'm an MP, an elected MP
My subjects are politically blind
I call them mere voters aka political customers
They're still innocent, naïve
They are valuable only during elections
I sometime pity them
They flock to freedom squares,
 In the scotching heat of the sun,
In tattered stained wears
Lips dry as bone,
Hunger engraved on their faces
Longing to listen to speeches from an MP
An MP that promises heaven and earth
Poor electoral materials!
Now that I got my hands on the funds,
What do I do with it?

By the way,
My youngest wife, Sandra Aguto nags me, non-stop
She is a pain in the neck
 She makes me sick
She "hi honeys" me for a car
She claims her friends ride Harriers
Why not her, an MP's?
She is sending me to grave
I must cancel this early journey
I'm going to buy her Toyota Wish

I'm an MP, an elected MP
My Land Cruiser is old
And my neighbor, Chol Sixty
Brags about his new Hummer
He thinks he is ahead of everyone
I am buying a train!!
Oh I'm forgetting
I'll add extra floors
To my 6-storey commercial glass building in Kileleshwa
My custodian, Ali Ngethi just called me
He has hired a contractor
A done deal!
Election Day comes in few days
What do I do?
Wait a minute
In my previous tenure;
I erected grass-thatched mud structures
Under the name of My-MP-For-Life primary school
 I also cleared three dirt roads
Now, I am going to buy chiefs and elders

Something that will keep discussions running smoothly
Cartons of Red Horse or Johnnie Walker will do
They will drink away suspicion of any kind
Two cans each
And they begin to sing and praise my name
Before they depart crawling, retarded
I'll ask them to
Allocate a land for constructing a health center
They can't hesitate to show me the piece of land
I sketch the premise
Enclose the area with barbwire
No, with bamboo poles
Barbwire is costly
Order excavation of foundation
Election is here
Oops! Sorry
I'm "re-re-elected"

Aluel

Aluel is a bright pupil
She is in her eighth grade
She has been at the top of her class since nursery school
She works out her school assignments perfectly
She likes science and social studies
She says she would like to be a radiologist in the future

Aluel is so disciplined
She never reports to school late
She has never missed out a single lesson
She respects both her teachers and fellow pupils alike

Aluel is a class prefect
She is a true role model
She dresses up smartly
Her uniforms are ever clean
She hardly quarrels
She talks to everyone nicely

Aluel is an orphan
Her father died in mysterious circumstances
Only the government knows
Her mother lost her life to malaria a couple of years ago
She has two younger siblings, both boys

Aluel stays at her uncle's place
Her uncle's family just moved to the city
She remains behind to take care of her blind
    grandmother
She cooks, she cleans,
She fetches water
She goes to the market

Aluel is so attractive
Her skin is so dark and shiny
Her physique, her eyes and her teeth are beyond
    description
Her smile is photic,
It could light up a dark room
In short, she is the younger version of Alek Wek

Aluel looks older than her age
She is kind of growing up in a rush

Her bosom is no longer normal,
Two strange dome-shaped objects are popping out
On her once bare chest
And they seem to be developing hour after hour
They are now at a 'grabbable' size

Aluel's Science teacher is behaving strange lately
He ogles her
He chats her up
He has even ceased to call Aluel by her name
He calls her 'Pion-pac'

Aluel is a child,
She lacks worldly experiences
Her teacher asks her to remain behind after school,
For a one-on-one important lesson
Aluel obeys
They sit at the corner of the room
A few minutes elapse,
The teacher introduces a different topic
He pulls down her bloomers,
Positions her on the desk,
And forces some hard thing between her legs

Aluel is in trouble
The pain is so unbearable
She lets out a deafening cry
Unfortunately, no one hears that,
She cries and begs him to stop it but he can't
Aluel faints
She gains consciousness hours later

She can't feel her waist, it's numb
But she manages to limp home

Aluel is absent from school today for the first time
But there is a problem at her class
Her classmates can't use their desks
They say it is hard to tell what exactly happened
But it looks like some sheep or,
Chicken got slaughtered on the desk
The teacher insists that it is just a red ink and,
Orders them to clean it up
Period!

Aluel is back to school, after a week
The teacher no longer smiles at her
He is moody
He browbeats her
Aluel gets confused
She can't understand why
She endures nevertheless

Aluel gets into trouble with her teacher
She reportedly failed a science test
Along with her three friends,
The teacher parades them before the class
With an 'uncle black', he whacks them in the bums
Aluel can't sit down, so are her friends
Coz the fall of the whip has done them much harm
The sight of their blood-stained uniforms,
Around the behinds tells it all
Aluel and friends are taken to the hospital,
To have their buts stitched

Aluel is at home, under a tree on a Saturday afternoon,
Doing revision
A neighbor, a married man with children comes by
He says he was good at math in school,
And he can show her some formulae
Aluel welcomes him
He is smelling alcohol though
A few minutes, he says he is thirsty and,
Asks Aluel to go get water from the house
He gets up and follows her

Aluel screams
Neighbors, mostly women, storm the compound,
To see what's going on
They learn of the crime
Authorities are informed
The man is beaten and dragged to the police station
Aluel is taken to the hospital

Aluel is at the hospital, seated on a bench,
Waiting for her turn to see a gynecologist
Her turn comes
She walks in
For the doc to practice his field,
Aluel must undress
After an hour of persuasion, she undresses
But Aluel's body is tempting and irresistible
What a gynecologist!

Aluel is in the hand of the authorities
Since there is no special center for housing the abused,

Aluel is at a police commissioner's home
His wives and children live in foreign cities
Foreign House helps do the cooking and cleaning
He is a 'nice' dude though
He clothes Aluel
He makes sure Aluel eats good food
Apparently, he shares his room with her

Aluel is sitting her final exams,
Commonly known as Certificate of Primary Education
After every paper,
She walks out of the exam room smiling

Aluel is unwell
She vomits, she shivers every morning
She notices that her abdomen is growing,
Her flat belly is losing flatness
It is showing
It's taking shape, D-shape

The Truth

What's truth?
What good is truth?
Who wants to hear the truth,
The whole truth,
And nothing but the truth?
Who says the truth?
What happens to those who speak the truth?
Why don't people want to hear the truth?
Where is the truth?

Truth is a quality or state of being true
It is a fact or belief that is accepted as true
Truth is that which is true
Or in accordance with facts or reality

Truth is of great value
It is precious
It is water, air and love
Truth is a key, it unlocks locks
It breaks codes and chains

It breaks barriers
Truth heals wounds
It builds, maintains bridges that connect people

Truth is not told by anyone
It is not told by eyewitnesses
Truth is never told by the popes, imams, paupers,
Members of Parliament, boys, girls or scientists
Neither is it told by detectives nor journalists
Truth is told by the truth itself

Truth hurts,
It is a thorn penetrating through a skin
Truth is ugly, no one falls for it
Truth is sulphuric acid, none wants to swallow it
Truth is a charging al-Qaeda suicide bomber, everyone
    runs away from it
Truth is a highly dangerous armed mad man, everyone
    hides from it

He who says the truth is shunned in the society
In a broad daylight, he's gunned down by hired thugs or
    police
A set up is hatched and when he gets caught, he's jailed,
    castrated and hanged
Or he is tortured badly and left to die
And his/her relatives are intimidated, harassed and
    imprisoned

Though no one wants to tell the truth,
Everyone wants to hear the truth

But truth is kept out of reach of you and me
It is a permanent resident of government's safe
Truth also lives under the carpet of a state house
It is in shackles, in private cages, serving unspecified
    term
It is kept in the dark, in the basement of a courthouse
Truth lies in your partner's handbag
It's somewhere in the ceilings of your house
Truth has money value, it is sold
Its buyers are rich businesspeople, politicians and
    religious leaders
Upon buying it, they flush it down the toilet

However, truth is indestructible
It's immortal
No matter what happens to the truth, it will always
    come to light,
With much more catastrophic effects

SOUTH SUDAN

My Country

PART I

South Sudan, a nation the whole world helped come
   into existence
But just to ironically bully it to death
Out of it, they squeeze breath
One quick instance is globalization
 It's rearing its ugly head into the baby nation,
Unnoticed
Say, jobs
Employment opportunities are being taken over by
   foreigners,
Distant ones
 Who are often introduced as diamantine experts
 Each with a work experience older than him/herself
 Don't get me wrong though
I am not xenophobic

And never shall I be
I hold nothing against them
 They made me what I am today
I work with them, every single day
They help me build my career day in day out
My worry is the bigger picture – South Sudan,
Its present and future
I am not a liberator
If you wanna give me a name,
Call me a messenger
What is going on right now is inequitable
It's unfair simply because South Sudan has nothing to
    offer in return
 Remember globalization is blood in blood out
Your nationals work in my country
And mine in yours
Period
I don't mean maize roasters
Not chapatti sellers
Nor tea-ladies
Nor boda-boda
No
I mean real service-givers,
Intellectuals
The doctors
Engineers
Weathermen
South Sudanese scholars are few
Majority have no work experience
 Just plain academic papers
And the silly and unhelpful

Socialist and capitalist theories
They foolishly hold on to so dearly
Ooh Karl Marx said this
Ooh Vladimir Lenin said that
With the experience-demand evidently used as
A ploy to demoralize and reject learned South Sudanese
From overseas varsities,
They return to foster-mother-countries
Where only manual labor is readily available to them
There, they are lumberjacks, dish-washers, waiter
    persons
When they actually have what it takes to be
Attorneys, physicians, accountants, environmentalists
    back home
This is not fair
And it looks like nothing will reverse it any soon
'Coz the supposed concerned souls are either
    unsurprisingly unaware
Or ignorant
Or busy,
Busy 'erecting their own huts'
Everyone for himself and God for us all
Seems to be the golden rule here
Day by day,
The international community gnaws South Sudan
Hour after hour,
Every foreigner bites off a big piece of the cakey Junub
Minute by minute,
The new nation is crumbling
It will be on its knees soon
But the whole world is always quick to deny it

'Oh we're helping you build it'
Helping my......
How do you help South Sudan when
You place the 5-year experience requirement
As a barrier?
How do you expect people who just accessed
    educational opportunities
To have five-year work experience?
Is that what you call help in your country?
This is not fair at all

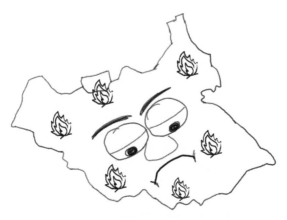

My Country

PART II

My country is odd, so odd
It's peopled with writers who do not write
Singers who do not sing
Rappers who do not rap
Journalists who not write journalese
Lawyers who do not practice legalese
Police officers who do not police
Leaders who do not lead,
Teachers who do not teach
Lecturers who do not lecture
Nurses who do not nurse
Farmers who do not farm
Name them

In my Country, everyone is everything
Ever girl is a supermodel

Every boy is a rapper
Everyone is a politician
Everyone knows everything
Everyone is a VIP,
Including those who have no idea what it stands for

My country is filthy rich, so rich.
Say, natural resources: oil, gold, wildlife, Teak.
However, everyone is a pauper
Everyone begs – yes everyone
All depends on handouts
So, where does this wealth go?
I don't know
He doesn't know
She doesn't know
Do you know?

My country is at peace, finally
But no one is secure,
Including the national figure number 1
No one goes out after dark
Each day is characterized by ethnic violence & rustling
Cattle raid in Bor,
Cattle raid in Pibor,
In Tonj
In Rumbek
In Budi
In Duk

My country is really odd
Sound of gunshots no longer scares nobody
'Coz it's been legitimized
Drive on Juba roads at your own risk
Bang!
Your car gets hit from behind
And two headless dudes spring out from the car that
    knocked yours,
Brandishing AK-47 riffles
And like a sack of onions, pull you out,
Slap you in the face until your ears begin to ring and
    vibrate like Nokia 3310
And press the two killing machines on each temple
If you don't wet your pants during this encounter, you're
    the man

In my country, anyone can become a millionaire
    overnight
Today, you meet a man in an old dirty smelly tattered
    button-less shirt,
With his dirty cracked feet seeking refuge in
    mismatching flip-flops, one blue one red
A week later, he's in a thousand dollar suits and riding a
    first-class V-8, his V-8
I love my country. It's odd,
So odd

Kiir Bullies Bashir

Last night, I had a dream
In my dream,
President Kiir visits his ailing partner,
President Omar Hassan Bashir
Bashir contracted diarrhea,
A chronic diarrhea
Coz he drank unclean water from river Nile
He couldn't afford bottled water
He is broke
Oil production got shutdown by Kiir

Bashir ekes out
Handouts from Arab League
After Kiir gave him emotional and moral strength,
He asks him what his say is
In regards to the outstanding CPA issues;
The Abyei,
Border issues,
Oil transit fees,
And nationality question
Before answering Kiir,
He gets up,
Runs to the toilet
Spends half an hour in there
He comes back,
Stands by the door,
And breathes heavily
It's here Kiir sees his full body frame
Silhouetting in an ankle-length loose white Jalabia
The beer-belly he acquired
Through South Sudan oil money shrinks;
It's disappearing
His ribs protrude
Kiir counts them
They're ten
Two of them got surgically removed
After he got shot by Kerubino Kuanyin Bol
During a one-on-one meeting somewhere in
    Omdurman
In the 90s,
An incident that went unreported for fear of
Grand official butchering of reporters

Along with their families
"I beg your pardon, repeat your question,
Ya baba Mayar", he asks Kiir
Before Kiir finishes shooting the same question for the
     second time,
Bashir dashes to the toilet again,
Leaving Kiir seething with rage;
Agitated,
Irritated
Kiir plunges into a sea of thoughts,
Trying to figure out how
He will make Bashir speak his language
Bashir comes back,
Holding a small bluish container
For keeping water used in place of toilet roll
He fills it up with water from an old pot
And places it near the door
He sits on an old mat
Made from reeds
People say his wife got the mat from a neighbor
Immediately after auctioneers
Stormed Bashir's house
And confiscated the furniture;
They were sent by the landlord
Who grew impatient
After Bashir failed to pay February rent
Back to the point:
Bashir begins to respond to Kiir
He starts off by telling Kiir to go to hell
'Cause he ain't letting any other thing
Slip through his fingers

Since he allowed south to go it alone as
An independent state through the 2011 referendum
Kiir begs him to reduce oil transit fee demand;
From $36 to 40 cents per barrel
Kiir also implores him to leave Abyei alone
But still, Bashir insists that Kiir goes to hell
And races to the toilet again
He spends his good time in there
Provoked by Bashir's attitude,
Kiir grows smarter
He hatches a plan
And waits till Bashir comes back
Salva says he wants to use the toilet
Bashir directs Kiir:
"Go straight on; turn left, turn left again.
It's the one with
 A green door next to the gate"
Salva leaves, taking along the Citizen Newspaper
He takes his time in there
Ten minutes elapse,
Still no sign of Kiir
Now the worst happens
Bashir gets pressed again;
Remember he has a running stomach
He rushes toward the toilet, the only toilet
Only to find it locked from inside
Salva is in, reading the newspaper
Atlala bara ya Salva. Ena taban
What are you doing in there?"
Bashir panics
But Kiir keeps mum

"Knock knock knock"
He knocks, he pushes the door
Kiir whistles
As he turns pages of the newspaper,
He scans through the stories
Pretending to find an interesting story to read
Finally, Kiir breaks the silence:
 "What do you think of my proposals?"
Bashir says they will discuss the issues back in the house
Kiir declines
And keeps reading the paper
Bashir begs Kiir, saying
"Please get out; I will sponsor 100 South Sudanese
　　university students"
Kiir says thanks but that's not what I want
With his left hand patting buttocks
And the right hand on the stomach;
Bashir begins to talk: "okay okay okay okay,
I'm proposing a meeting with you, just two us.
And it will be mediated by Obama himself"
Kiir resumes whistling
"Kiir please let me use the latrine,
Don't let me do it in my pants
Kiir you are causing a scene;
My wives and kids are milling around
And I can see my neighbors peering
I'll do anything you want me to.
I will return all the barrels I confiscated,
 I've given up Abyei. I...
 ... Ding... dong... Ding...dong,
My mobile phone rang,
Waking me from the dream

Your River, My River

Your river is perpetual,
It's older than time itself

Mine is a passer-by,
It's a passing wind

Your river is long
Mine is tall

Yours has no oculi but it sees
Mine has a pair, but it sees not

Your river flows
Mine walks

Yours is filled with colorless liquid
Mine with reddish liquid

Your river ripples
Mine squelches

Your river kills
Mine too
Yours drowns
Mine executes

Your river is home to crocodiles, Chironex fleckeri
Mine shelters unintelligence, ignorance and thievery

Generous is your river,
A million lives depend on it
So selfish is mine,
It cares for selected few

Your river is called Iteru
Mine is called…?

Acknowledgment

This book wouldn't have been possible without Martha Akuany Mabiei, who happens to be my mother. She once threatened me, saying: "If you think you go to school for me, then stop going to school." This was after I threatened to drop out of high school if she didn't buy me Timbaland boots. "Where do you think I can get 7,000 Ksh?" She asked.

This is for Thon-da (Isaac Thon), who exposed me to books at tender age.

This is for Uncle Ayuen Madit Dhol, whose books I used to sniff at the age of two or three.

And this is for all my friends and cousins, who have been nudging me to get published, namely:

Lydia Gai

Ayen Martin Awan

Zack Mayul

Kayole AD

Malueth Kuol

Lightning Source UK Ltd.
Milton Keynes UK
UKHW010649080321
379980UK00002B/521

9 780648 929161